Raymond Burke

The Metaphoric Manual

The Drouth
CCA
350 Sauchiehall Street
Glasgow, Scotland
G2 3JD

First published 2021

ISBN 978-1-80068-009-8 The Metaphoric Manual (paperback)

Burke, Raymond

All rights reserved. No part of this publication may be reproduced, distributed, or transmitted in any form or by any means, including photocopying, recording, or other electronic or mechanical methods, without the prior written permission, except in the case of brief quotations embodied in critical reviews and certain other noncommercial uses permitted by copyright law.

Literary examples quoted within the text are within the public domain and are included for educational purposes. Any errors or misattributions will be rectified in subsequent editions.

The Metaphoric Manual

© Raymond Burke 2021

First Edition

raymondburke007@gmail.com

Thanks to - Johnny Rodger, Richard McLean, Denize McKernan

Contents

Introduction – 5

Tropes – 9
- Figures of Similitude – 10
- Figures of Association – 33
- Figures of Exaggeration – 48
- Figures of Personification – 55

Ironies – 67
- Figures of Understatement – 68
- Figures of Opposition – 80
- Figures of Ambiguity – 88

Schemes – 91
- Figures of Repetition – 92
- Figures of Parallelism – 112
- Figures of Disruption – 122
- Figures of Omission and Sharing – 131

Figures of Sound – 139
- Repeated Sounds – 140
- Discrete Sound – 149

Functional Glossary – 153

Works Quoted – 157

Index of Figures – 161

To Concha

Introduction

'The chief praise and cunning of our poet is in the discrete use of his figures, as the skilful painters is in the good conveyance of his colours and shadowing traits of his pencil, with a delectable variety, by all measure and just proportion, and in places most aptly to be bestowed.'
George Puttenham (1589)

The purpose of this book is to introduce teachers, students and all lovers of literature to the most popular and useful literary devices employed by great writers over the centuries. These are commonly referred to as 'figures of speech' and are presented in the main body of this work in four sections: Tropes, Schemes, Ironies and Figures of Sound. In tropes, meaning is changed, in schemes, the grammar or order is disturbed or manipulated for effect, ironies are cases of double meaning or opposition, and figures of sound are the devices in which sound is used to foreground words and ideas.

The problem with other collections of figures of speech is that the figures are usually buried within an eclectic array of literary terms, rhetoric, theories and poetic forms, and these are more often than not presented in alphabetical order with only a single example of each device if any. Consequently, when a reader encounters an interesting figurative technique in a text, it is incredibly difficult to find any further information without trudging through countless dictionaries of terms in the hope of eventually stumbling across the correct entry. Indeed, the inclusion of certain important figures and even the actual meanings vary from book to book and, as usual, searching the web is a minefield of confusion and contradiction. At the other end of the scale, simplified lists of figures are often displayed on colourful classroom posters with arbitrary inclusions and exclusions. There are always the teachers' favourites, simile and metaphor, but rarely devices as important and useful as metonymy. Alliteration is universal, but litotes, a device used on a daily basis by millions, is not at all ubiquitous in the classroom. As a result of all this, the reader is left with either too much information or too little. This book aims to solve that problem by presenting the most useful and popular figures grouped logically in relationship to one another. Several examples of each figure are also included to show how the device is used by different writers and provide teachers with a valuable resource.

How to use this book

The first part and main body of this book collects related figures within sections. Each figure is explained in detail and followed by several quotations from literature and popular culture. Therefore, when a student is studying a particular device, they can go, via the alphabetical index, to the main entry for a detailed explanation and a few examples of the device in use. Some study of the nearby related figures will also serve to increase the student's understanding.

Also included is a glossary of figures by function. When a reader stumbles upon an unknown but interesting device being used in a text - for example: repeated words - the functional glossary can be used to find all of the figures of repetition listed together which will then enable them to pinpoint the exact device being used. This can then be followed to the main entry on that device for a more detailed description and further examples.

The book can also be used in creative writing workshops by opening the book at a random figure and challenging the participants to adapt the examples and produce their own. (Although it would be inadvisable to try metalepsis or catachresis in the first lesson.)

Format of main entries

Each figure is presented in bold capitals with its pronunciation in brackets underneath and a brief description of the function:

> **METONYMY**
> (meh TOH ni mi)
> *Representation by association*

Quotations

Although this book contains many famous literary lines, maxims and sayings, it should not be seen as merely a book of quotations. The examples included have been selected because of their artistic form rather than moral value. However, by chance, or more probably by design, most of history's greatest speeches also employ history's greatest figures of speech and consequently many well known quotations are included.

Punctuation and Presentation

Literary examples are presented in single quote marks followed by the author's surname and the title of the work in italics:

> 'Better to reign in Hell than serve in Heaven.'
> Milton, *Paradise Lost*

Multiple lines of poetry are presented without quote marks:

> How like a winter hath my absence been,
> From thee the pleasure of the fleeting year!
> Shakespeare, *Sonnet XCVII*

Or with quote marks and line breaks:

> 'I met Murder on the way/ He had a mask like Castlereagh.'
> Shelley, *The Mask of Anarchy*

For the sake of aesthetics, if clauses or phrases are clear enough without ellipsis marks (…) at the beginning or end, they will be omitted and the clause presented as a shorter sentence.

Terminology

The analytical terminology of tropes can be confusing. In his study of metaphor, I. A. Richards refers to the constituent parts as 'tenor' and 'vehicle'. Unfortunately, for many students, these terms lack clarity and it is therefore much more helpful to use the stylistic tradition of 'target' and 'source'. Target = tenor / Source = vehicle. The 'target' is whatever is to be enhanced by the trope and the 'source' is where we borrow the new qualities or aspects to be compared. Consequently, these are the terms that are used for the main tropes and throughout this work.

The Metaphoric Table

This book owes its existence to the popularity of the Metaphoric Table wall-chart. Whilst in conversation with some students in Stirling University a few years ago, I accepted the challenge to produce a diagram which would give a graphic representation of the relationships between some tropes we had just discussed in an English seminar. The idea was to investigate the relationships between the most popular figures and present the results visually. Unsurprisingly, as each device was researched, several others cropped up. Consequently, what was initially intended to be a chart of less than twenty figures quickly grew to more than fifty.

    The most obvious format to present such a variety of terms was science's Periodic Table. There are, indeed, such tables of everything from cats to Star Trek; there are even some that list figures of speech: however, these merely mimic the design without bothering about logical representation. Therefore, rather than simply including the usual jumble of terms in the aesthetic style of the Periodic Table, priority is given to logical relationships between the terms. The Metaphoric Table is the result. In the same way as the Periodic Table presents elements, the Metaphoric Table presents figures alongside or in close proximity to other related figures for quick reference. For instance, if looking for the name of a literary technique of disruption used in a work, each closely related device can be examined to find the precise description. On the chart, tropes are presented in light blue boxes, ironies in green, schemes in yellow and figures of sound in red. Each entry provides a brief explanation of the function of each device and a few examples from literature. The Metaphoric Table can be used independently or in conjunction with this Metaphoric Manual.

The Metaphoric Manual

Tropes

Tropes are figures of speech which are non-literal. Indeed the word trope comes from the Greek 'to turn or convert'. They compare unusual aspects, exaggerate, transfer meaning or represent by association.

Figures of Similitude
Simile, Metaphor

SIMILE
(SIH-mi-leh)
Qualities compared in two unrelated things

Simile is the most common of all the tropes. It is a figure in which two distinct things are explicitly compared: 'She was as pretty as a daffodil' or 'He had a face like a Halloween cake.' The qualities, aspects or attributes of one thing are shared with another.

Although many textbooks describe simile as a comparison that always includes 'like' or 'as', this is a neglectful oversimplification. Younger students can be confused by this lethargic classification; many sentences contain 'like' or 'as' without being similes, and many actual similes use other terminology such as 'resembled', 'seemed' or 'akin to'. In Dickens' *David Copperfield*, we find: 'He reminded me of an ugly and rebellious genie'; which is clearly a simile, whereas cases such as 'I like a wee whisky' or 'we visited Salamanca as well as Madrid', are not. Therefore, when teaching simile, the tutor should focus primarily on the creativity of the comparison with more attention being paid to the qualities and aspects shared. The forms and syntax of similes exemplified throughout this book can then be reserved for scaffolding.

One of the best known similes in literature is:

'My love is like a red, red rose.'
Robert Burns, *Red Red Rose*

Here, two discrete things are being compared, 'love' and 'rose'; implied qualities are carried across from the latter to the former. Burns enhances the image of his love with the perceived qualities of the flower: natural, beautiful, fragile. In a more exaggerated example:

'My heart is like a singing bird.'
Rossetti, *A Birthday*

Rossetti enhances the emotions in her heart with qualities associated with a singing bird: beauty, joy, fragility, etc. As with love and the rose, the heart and the bird are unrelated. Similes should always link unrelated things. (However, there is an exception to this rule when comparing people with fictional or historical characters: 'He behaved like Nero', 'She was as beautiful as a princess'.)

Another point that is often overlooked is what actually distinguishes simile from literal comparison. Simile is not merely an expression or confirmation of sameness, it is an imaginative, creative manipulation of perceived similarity. In an artistic sense, it is something contrived rather than acknowledged. For instance, if there are two twins, Craig and Charlie and someone says 'Craig looks like Charlie' - this is not a simile - it is only an expression of similarity. On the other hand, if someone says 'Craig and Charlie are like two peas in a pod', then that is a simile. To produce a true simile there is a creative process of finding similarity in aspects of two distinct and unrelated things.

Target	Source	Aspects
Heart	Singing bird	Natural, happy, carefree
Love	Red Rose	Beautiful, precious
Craig and Charlie	Peas in a pod	Visually identical

Idiomatic similes

As time passes, many similes become idiomatic shorthand for commonly agreed ideas: 'like water off a duck's back', 'like a red rag to a bull', 'like looking for a needle in a haystack', 'as hard as nails', 'as quiet as mice', 'as fit as a dray horse'. These phrases have been part of everyday speech for so long that they have become cliché. However, although they should be avoided within the narrative voice of a text, they can be quite useful for natural sounding dialogue between everyday characters. Indeed, in *David Copperfield*, Charles Dickens acknowledges this simplistic style when describing one character: 'As good as gold and as true as steel - those were her similes'; Dickens thus diminishes the individuality of the character by her adherence to such clichés.

Categorisation of similes

As discussed above, most, but by no means all, similes use 'like' or 'as'. There are several forms, each with its own particular purpose. Therefore, when we want to create a new simile it is advantageous to know and understand the different possibilities that are available to us. This will then help writers and students focus on whichever aspects of their targets they wish to enhance. Targets of similes can be nouns, verbs, adjectives or even adverbs. Similes are categorised as follows:

Main Types of Simile

1	Standard 'like'	Noun 'like'
		Verb 'like'
		Phrasal verb 'like'
		Noun and verb phrase 'like'
2	Double 'As'	Target - as - adjective/ adverb - as
3	Single 'As'	Omitted 'as' from double
		'As' synonymous with like
		'As if', 'as though'
4	Suffixed	Noun + 'like' becomes adjective
5	Variations	Using neither 'like' nor 'as'
6	Extended simile	Multiple aspects compared

Type 1 Standard 'like' similes

Standard 'like' similes are the least complicated and use nouns or verbs as targets. For example, in the sentence, 'Brian's guitar was like a lethal weapon', the target is the guitar and the source is the lethal weapon. The qualities of danger and threat are carried over to the target. These basic noun or pronoun similes can be presented as:

Target - **like** - source.

Noun/ Pronoun 'like' Similes:

'He was a tall thin man with a nose like a beak.'
Doyle, *The Hound of the Baskervilles*

'A chest like the heave of a hill.'
  Brown, *The House with the Green Shutters*

'With eyes like carbuncles, the hellish Pyrrhus
Old grandsire Priam seeks.'
  Shakespeare, *Hamlet*

'Her voice… like an old-fashioned coffee grinder.'
  Runyon, *Neat Strip*

'The sky was like a vast flat wall of cobalt, with roofs
and spires of black paper pasted upon it.'
  Orwell, *Down and Out in Paris and London*

'In the eastern sky there was a yellow patch like a rug
laid for the feet of the coming sun.'
  Crane, *The Red Badge of Courage*

'I was like Daniel in the den of lions.'
  Hogg, *Confessions of a Justified Sinner*

'We are like lambs in a field, disporting themselves under
the eye of the butcher.'
  Schopenhauer, *On the Suffering of the World*

'He was like a cock who thought the sun had risen to
hear him crow.'
  Eliot, *Adam Bede*

The structure of noun similes need not always follow the target-like-source framework. On occasion, 'like' is placed before the source and target:

How like a winter hath my absence been,
From thee the pleasure of the fleeting year!
  Shakespeare, *Sonnet XCVII*

And like the sun borne to its polar hell,
My heart is no more than a red, frozen block.
  Baudelaire, *Song of Autumn*

Verb 'like' Similes

In noun 'like' similes, targets and subjects are one and the same. However, verbs can also be targets and are usually structured thus:

Subject - **Target verb** - Like - Source

'Oscar remained like a rock left by the ebbing sea.'
Macpherson, *Ossian*

'The twinges that sting like needles his legs and neck.'
Whitman, *Song of Myself*

There's a certain slant of light, / On winter afternoons,
That oppresses, like the weight / Of cathedral tunes.
Dickinson, *There's A Certain Slant Of Light*

'The kitten which had scrambled up her back and stuck like a burr just out of reach.'
Alcott, *Little Women*

'He desired I would stand like a Colossus.'
Swift, *Gulliver's Travels*

As with noun similes, the syntax of verb similes need not be rigid and the verb may be placed after the comparison:

'And like a thunderbolt he falls.'
Tennyson, *The Eagle*

'Till death like sleep might steal on me.'
Shelley, *Stanzas Written in Dejection*

'Like washable beaver hats that improve with rain, his nerves were rendered stouter and more vigorous by showers of tears.'
Dickens, *Oliver Twist*

'But there dropt words from you last night and this morning that, like sparks from flint, showed the metal within.'
Scott, *Ivanhoe*

Verb Simile Characterisation

In the preceding similes the verbs are the main target, but this kind of comparison can also be employed to carry the connotations of a source verb to a character subject. For example, in *Catriona,* a young girl is described:

'She walked like a young deer, and stood like a birch upon the mountainside.'
Stevenson, *Catriona*

Obvious qualities of the deer: healthy, proud, part of nature, etc. are shared through the target verb action to the subject. In the following examples, characters are painted using the same technique:

'He sat blinking like an owl.'
Buchan, *The Thirty-Nine Steps*

'His grey whiskers bristled like those of an angry cat.'
Doyle, T*he Hound of the Baskervilles*

'She trembled all over and shook like a white narcissus.'
Wilde, *The Picture of Dorian Gray*

'Into those sodden woeful households she entered like a spring wind.'
Buchan, *Witch Wood*

"I am sure," said Uriah, writhing himself into the silence like a conger-eel, "that this is a subject full of unpleasantness to everybody."
Dickens, *David Copperfield*

'[The doctor] fled out of the door like a detected thief.'
Stevenson, *The Body-Snatcher*

'We saw her run... and melt into the city's strife and sound, like a dewdrop in an ocean.'
Dickens, *Bleak House*

'Tess still stood hesitating like a bather about to make his plunge.'
Hardy, *Tess of the d'Urbervilles*

Phrase Target Similes

Quite often, rather than using a single word for comparison, a much wider target is required. It can be observed in the following examples that phrases are being compared:

Noun Phrases:

'A hideous old general, with a mouth of false teeth like a pianoforte too full of keys.'
Dickens, *Bleak House*

'These three words from her were in a flash like the glitter of a drawn blade.'
James, *The Turn of the Screw*

'The dim roar of London was like the bourdon note of a distant organ.'
Wilde, *The Picture of Dorian Gray*

'The faces below him, set, composed, awful in their decency, seemed like a stone wall against which he must beat with feeble hands.'
Buchan, *Witch Wood*

'Her face… was all puckers and creases, like a shrivelled red apple.'
Joyce, *Dubliners*

Verb Phrases:

'It shines in his vocabulary like a jewel in a muck-heap.'
Stevenson, *The Treasure of Franchard*

'His head kept turning to left and right with two bright little twinkling eyes, like a mouse when he ventures out from his hole.'
Doyle, *The Sign of Four*

'Shaking the water from her black locks like a Skye terrier escaped from his bath.'
Eliot, *The Mill on the Floss*

'Her frail soul, tormenting itself in its invincible ignorance like a small bird beating about the cruel wires of a cage.'
Conrad, *Lord Jim*

'To follow her thought was like following a voice which speaks too quickly to be taken down by one's pencil.'
Woolf, *To the Lighthouse*

Phrasal Verb Similes:

'Its four bare walls seemed to close in upon you like the sides of a coffin.'
O Henry, *The Skylight Room*

'His boot toes were turned sharply up, in the fashion of the day, like sleigh-runners.'
Twain, *Tom Sawyer*

'If you put her in a room with someone, up went her back like a cat's; or she purred.'
Woolf, *Mrs Dalloway*

Adjectives or Adverbs with a verb target:

Subject - **Target verb** - **Adjective** - Like - Source

'He rose, unsteady, long, pale, indistinct, like a vapour exhaled by the earth.'
Conrad, *Heart of Darkness*

Subject - **Target verb** - **Adverb** - Like - Source

'She and the girl spoke rapidly together, their tongues moving quickly like those of two serpents.'
O Henry, *Sisters of the Golden Circle*

'The corners of her mouth went down suddenly like a barometer.'
O Henry, *Between Rounds*

2 Double 'as' Similes

Adjectives and adverbs may also be the main focus for similes. Rather than saying: 'he was like a mountain', the writer may want to focus on a particular adjectival quality and rephrase the simile: 'he was as big as a mountain'. As an alternative to the verb-simile: 'she ran like a gazelle', an adverb could be introduced instead to produce: 'she ran as quickly as a gazelle'. Since the adjectives and adverbs are enclosed within the repeated 'as', these can be categorised as Double 'as' similes.

Adjective Similes:

> Target - as - **adjective** - as - source

'Her eyes sparkled as bright as diamonds.'
    Brontë, *Wuthering Heights*

'The boy remained as dismal as a hearse.'
    Twain, *Tom Sawyer*

'This hand/ As soft as dove's down and as white as it.'
    Shakespeare, *The Winter's Tale*

'He is a born leader of men, and as brave as a lion.'
    Buchan, *Prester John*

'Alan was as ready as a loaded musket.'
    Stevenson, *Catriona*

'Linton's [soul] is as different as a moonbeam from lightning, or frost from fire.'
    Brontë, *Wuthering Heights*

The same form is often used in sarcasm: 'as clear as mud', 'as useful as a chocolate teapot'.

'His countenance bore as little the marks of self-denial as his habit indicated contempt for worldly splendour.'
    Scott, *Ivanhoe*

The Double 'as' can also enclose 'much' in combination with a preceding verb:

'I sneezed almost as much as if Salem House had been a great snuff box.'
    Dickens, *David Copperfield*

Adverb Similes:

> Target verb - as - **adverb** - as - source

'There was no end to his questions; he put them as earnestly as a child.'
    Stevenson, *Kidnapped*

'They mingle as easily as two brooklets that ask for nothing but to entwine themselves and ripple with ever-interlacing curves in the leafiest hiding-places.'
    Eliot, *Adam Bede*

'He slept as soundly as if the roaring of cannon were his ordinary lullaby.'
    Dickens, *The Pickwick Papers*

'Men's lives are as thoroughly blended with each other as the air they breathe: evil spreads as necessarily as disease.'
    Eliot, *Adam Bede*

3 Single 'as' Similes

3a   Single 'as' - One Omitted

The same effect as the Double 'as' can be achieved by simply omitting the first. For instance, the sentence: 'It was as lonely as a lighthouse' can easily be rephrased: 'It was lonely as a lighthouse'.

> Target - **adjective** - as - source

'The illusion was transient as lightning.'
    Hardy, *Tess of the d'Urbervilles*

'I wandered lonely as a cloud that floats on high o'er vales and hills.'
    Wordsworth, *Daffodils*

'All the others stood firm and motionless, as the grey stones that lay scattered on the heath around them.'
Scott, *Old Mortality*

'Prejudices, it is well known, are most difficult to eradicate from the heart whose soil has never been loosened or fertilised by education: they grow there, firm as weeds among stones.'
Brontë, *Jane Eyre*

3b Single 'as' - synonymous with 'like'
When a single 'as' is used in a simile, it is often a synonym for 'like'. The following examples could just as easily be written with 'like' in place of 'as':

'They take suggestion as cats lap milk.'
Shakespeare, *The Tempest*

'She dealt with moral problems as a cleaver deals with meat.'
Joyce, *Dubliners*

'Formerly, his heart had been as a locked casket with its treasure inside.'
Eliot, *Silas Marner*

'My heart wept for the sight of Olalla as a child weeps for its mother.'
Stevenson, *Olalla*

'I am as one dead for years.'
Runyon, *Old Em's Kentucky Home*

3c Single 'as' - 'as if', 'as though'
Another form of simile with close synonymity to 'like' makes use of the conjunctions, 'as if' and 'as though' for comparisons:

'I had seen the damp lying on the outside of my little window, as if some goblin had been crying there all night, and using the window for a pocket-handkerchief.'
Dickens, *Great Expectations*

'He threw off intonations as if he were tossing roses.'
James, *The Turn of the Screw*

'A stiff brown wig that looked as if it were made of gingerbread.'
Dickens, *David Copperfield*

'Nonsense, nonsense, she said to herself, more and more gently as if this beauty, this scent, this colour and Mrs Pym trusting her, were a wave which she let flow over her.'
Woolf, *Mrs Dalloway*

'She was a curious woman, whose dresses always looked as if they had been designed in a rage and put on in a tempest.'
Wilde, *The Picture of Dorian Gray*

'He felt as though he were wandering in the forests of the sea bottom.'
Orwell, *Nineteen Eighty-Four*

'It was as though a veil had been rent.'
Conrad, *Heart of Darkness*

'She hung upon Estella's beauty, hung upon her words, hung upon her gestures, and sat mumbling her own trembling fingers while she looked at her, as though she were devouring the beautiful creature she had reared.'
Dickens, *Great Expectations*

4 Suffixed 'Like' Adjective

Another way of using 'like' in a simile is by simply suffixing it to a noun to make an adjective. This creates curtal or abbreviated similes without disrupting the flow of the text.

'A lean, ferret-like man, furtive and sly looking was waiting for us on the platform.'
Doyle, *The Boscombe Valley Mystery*

'Her binding proceeds with clock-like monotony.'
Hardy, *Tess of the d'Urbervilles*

'Or waiting dead-like till my spirit arouses me'
Whitman, *Song of Myself*

'But leechlike to their fainting country cling.'
Shelley, *England in 1819*

'That capability and god-like reason.'
Shakespeare, *Hamlet*

'For the first time Lydgate was feeling the hampering threadlike pressure of small social conditions.'
Eliot, *Middlemarch*

These constructs can appear somewhat archaic and indeed many similar constructions have, throughout the years, gradually had their the suffixes shortened from '-like' to '-ly'. These now form adjectives such as beggarly, sickly, cowardly, and adverbs such as slowly, angrily, meekly.

5 Variations - Similes that use neither 'like' nor 'as'

A wide variety of similes function without the use of 'like' or 'as'. There are many alternatives such as conjunctions with comparative verbs that can be adapted to suit the writer's own style and requirements. For instance, the conjunction 'than' is often used following a comparative:

Than Similes:

Comparative - than - source

'It [the night] is darker than a yard down a bear's throat.'
Runyon, *Barbecue*

'The lark was never gayer than that excellent woman.'
Dickens, *David Copperfield*

'And duller shouldst thou be than the fat weed
That roots itself in ease on Lethe wharf.'
Shakespeare, *Hamlet*

Each of the preceding examples could be adapted into Double 'as' similes. However, using the comparative with 'than' gives them an extra degree of amplification. There are also many similes that combine 'more' with 'than'.

> 'I knew no more of my descent than any cadger's dog.'
> Stevenson, *Kidnapped*

> 'To tear treasure out of the bowels of the land was their desire, with no more moral purpose at the back of it than there is in burglars breaking into a safe.'
> Conrad, *Heart of Darkness*

Countless other similes are constructed without the need of 'like' or 'as', a selection of which are listed below:

Compare:
'This task, which might be compared to spurring a tired jade, or to hammering upon cold iron.'
> Scott, *Ivanhoe*

Imagine:
'If you want a picture of the future, imagine a boot stamping on a human face - for ever.'
> Orwell, *Nineteen Eighty-Four*

Manner of:
'So they go out in a loose procession, something after the manner of a straggling funeral.'
> Dickens, *Bleak House*

Might have been:
'In an office that might have been on the ground floor of the Tower of Babel.'
> Dickens, *David Copperfield*

Remind:
'She reminds me more than somewhat of a woodpecker that someone knocks out of a tree with a rock.'
> Runyon, *Little Pinks*

Resemble:
'His deep-set bile-shot eyes, and the high thin fleshless nose gave him somewhat the resemblance to a fiery bird of prey.'
 Doyle, *The Speckled Band*

'Clavers turned his deep grey eye upon them, which more than the eye of any human being resembled that of a serpent.'
 Hogg, *The Brownie of Bodsbeck*

Seem:
'Her hands seemed to be made of cool ivory.'
 Wilde, *The Picture of Dorian Gray*

'University as a step to anything but ordination seemed, to this man of fixed ideas, a preface without a volume.'
 Hardy, *Tess of the D'Urbervilles*

Should have been:
'He disclosed among his toothless gums a few such fangs as should have been a dog's or rat's.'
 Dickens, *Oliver Twist*

So:
'Her words faded. So a rocket fades.'
 Woolf, *Mrs Dalloway*

Suggest:
'Little two-storey houses… which were somehow curiously suggestive of rat-holes.'
 Orwell, *Nineteen Eighty-Four*

Each of the preceding examples could easily be translated into a much simpler similaic format, but perhaps the writers' art is better appreciated by leaving them as they are, and as a reminder not to be misled by the 'only-like-or-as' brigade.

6 Extended Similes

For the sake of clarity and brevity, most of the previous examples are syntactically uncomplicated. The qualities shared and compared are obvious even if at times quite extreme. However, some of the most artistic and memorable uses of simile arise when the author extends the figure to explain the source or enhance the comparison.

'The place, with its grey sky and withered garlands, its bared spaces and scattered dead leaves, was like a theatre after the performance - all strewn with crumpled playbills.'
James, *The Turn of the Screw*

'He was now, with respect to his fortune, like a rider who has flung his reins on the horse's neck, and while he abandoned himself to circumstances, was at least, relieved from the task of attempting to direct them.'
Scott, *Old Mortality*

'The kindness fell on him as sunshine falls on the wretched — he had no heart to taste it, and felt that it was very far off him.'
Eliot, *Silas Marner*

'Overcome by his own grief, which rose like a moon looked at from a terrace, ghastly, beautiful with light from the sunken day.'
Woolf, *Mrs Dalloway*

'Women have served all these centuries as looking glasses possessing the magic and delicious power of reflecting the figure of man at twice its natural size.'
Woolf, *A Room of One's Own*

Although, as previously stated, worn-out phrases should generally be avoided, they can still, on occasion, be useful to prompt new ideas or responses. This is a standard technique in comedy, where the initial clichéd simile is merely a set up for the revelation of the unexpected attributes of the source. For example, it would be lazy to use such a tired phrase as 'You're like a broken record,' unless you follow it with 'round and cracked'. A short clarifying explanation can also be added when creating proverbs such as Bacon's: 'Money is like muck, not good except it be spread.'

'His family is as old as the hills and infinitely more respectable.'
Dickens, *Bleak House*

"It hurts my feelings, especially," he says, "when I am as honest as the day is long."
"The days are getting shorter."
Runyon, *Barbecue*

The structure and forms of simile in this chapter are presented primarily to provide examples and templates for teachers and students. However, it should always be made clear that the true art is in the creativity of comparison rather than the use of specific structures or words. As with all of the figures in this book, the real challenge is to create new, unexpected and vivid ideas.

METAPHOR
(MEH ta for)
One thing described in terms of another

Whereas simile is a self-evident literal comparison, metaphor, as an individual figure, presents us with a non-literal transference of identity. Metaphor is a much stronger trope as the idea is transferred from one thing to another rather than simply being compared. No longer would the poet's muse be described as being 'like' a red rose; if metaphor is employed, his love then 'is' a red rose. This form, known as 'direct metaphor', is grammatically and semantically close to simile as it includes the target. However, this is not the case with 'implied metaphor' where, unlike simile, the target need not be included. Metaphors may also be 'extended' to describe further corresponding attributes of the images. Other types include 'dead metaphor' where meaning has been lost by overuse and 'mixed metaphor' where it has been used in error. (see catachresis)

Main Types of Metaphor

Direct	Target and source
Implied	Source without target
Extended	Target and source with extended aspects

Type 1 - Direct Metaphor

Direct metaphor is the closest in form to simile and accordingly both target and source are included. For example, in the sentence, 'Tom's desk was a disaster zone', 'Tom's desk' is the target, and 'disaster zone' is the source. Aspects of chaos and disorder are thus transferred to the desk. Taking an example from literature:

'Advertising is the rattling of a stick inside a swill-bucket.'
Orwell, *Keep the Aspidistra Flying*

Orwell could just as easily have written 'Advertising is like…' but the image would have been much weaker.

Direct Metaphor

Target	Source	Aspects
Advertising	Swill-bucket stick	Noise, revulsion, pigs
Tom's desk	Disaster zone	Mess, chaos

The simplest form of direct metaphor includes 'be' verbs:

Target - **'be' verb** - source

'The curves of her throat were the curves of a white lily.'
Wilde, *The Picture of Dorian Gray*

'I ardently hope that the gratification of your wishes may not be a serpent to sting you.'
Shelley, *Frankenstein*

'Those who shine most in private company, are but secondary stars in the constellation of genius.'
Smollett, *The Expedition of Humphry Clinker*

'He's a leech in his dispositions, he's a screw and vice in his actions, a snake in his twistings and a lobster in his claws.'
Dickens, *Bleak House*

Direct metaphors without 'be' verb

'The breaking of the billows of the restless sea of life.'
   Dickens, *The Pickwick Papers*

'Snagsby... lays upon the table half-a-crown: that magic balsam of his for all kinds of wounds.'
   Dickens, *Bleak House*

'A room which... looked out on a cobbled yard and a forest of chimney pots.'
   Orwell, *Nineteen Eighty-Four*

'Look, he's winding up the watch of his wit; by-and-by it will strike.'
   Shakespeare, *The Tempest*

Metaphor using other parts of speech

The preceding examples all have nouns as targets but other parts of speech may also be used:

Adjectives:

'I saw a cadaverous face appear at a small window.'
   Dickens, *David Copperfield*

'It was a very narrow street - a ravine of tall, leprous houses.'
   Orwell, *Down and Out in Paris and London*

Verbs:

'My heart quaked with terror.'
   Hogg, *Confessions of a Justified Sinner*

'Upon which the young man, looking round, instantly evaporates.'
   Dickens, *Bleak House*

'My earlier operations were crowned with a full measure of success.'
   Stevenson, *The Wrecker*

Type 2 - Implied Metaphor

In implied metaphor the target is not necessary. If we rewrite our previous example, 'Tom's desk was a disaster zone' as 'Tom sat typing at his disaster zone', the qualities of mess and chaos are still present but the reader would now have to work out that the disaster zone is Tom's desk. The target is thus implied rather than directly stated. When Stevenson writes of Dr Jekyll, 'I have been doomed to such a dreadful shipwreck', the reader must imagine, considering the wider context of the story, which aspects of a shipwreck can be transferred to Jekyll's life.

Implied Metaphor

Unstated Target	Source	Aspects
Jekyll's life	Shipwreck	Loss, solitude, hopelessness
Tom's desk	Disaster zone	Mess, chaos

Although the reader has to determine the target, the effect is much more intense as it is created in a single word.

At times, the target can be deciphered easily:

'These strong Egyptian fetters I must break.'
    Shakespeare, *Anthony and Cleopatra*

'To tear treasure out of the bowels of the land was their desire.'
    Conrad, *Heart of Darkness*

'Mr Bucket, who has seen through the transparency of Mrs Snagsby's vinegar at a glance...'
    Dickens, *Bleak House*

At other times, implied metaphors can be a little more difficult to unravel:

'The customers know very well that Chester is only fighting some parasol.' (a boxer who will fold up.)
    Runyon, *Leopard's Spots*

> 'No difference in this respect between the base metals and the precious.' (poor/ nobility.)
> Dickens, *Bleak House*

> 'This chain of flowers you have taken up is very easily broken, or it might become a chain of lead.' (very young couple becoming engaged.)
> Dickens, *Bleak House*

As has been shown with these examples, implied metaphor brings the image sharply into focus. The brevity of this form means that it is also much more difficult to translate to simile.

Type 3 - Extended Metaphor

Metaphors need not be restricted to single words and short phrases. They frequently include longer explanations of the aspects and qualities being transferred. This is known as 'extended' or 'sustained' metaphor. This allows the writer to justify the image or expand the idea creatively. Simple extensions can produce short aphorisms and proverbs:

> 'Treachery and violence are spears pointed at both ends; they wound those who resort to them worse than their enemies.'
> Brontë, *Wuthering Heights*

> 'If man makes himself a worm, he must not complain when he is trodden on.'
> Immanuel Kant

> 'Let the old tree wither... so the stately hope of the forest be preserved.'
> Scott, *Ivanhoe*

> 'I will watch with the wiliness of a snake, that I may sting with its venom.'
> Shelley, *Frankenstein*

An extended metaphor can also be sustained over several sentences, paragraphs or even throughout the entire work. For example, in *Bleak House* the clients of a powerful, but recently deceased, lawyer are presented as his coach horses:

> 'He held all these horses in his hand, and could have drove them his own way, I haven't a doubt; but he got fetched off the box head-foremost, and now they have got their legs over the traces, and are all dragging and pulling their own ways.'
> Dickens, *Bleak House*

In the following extended metaphors, love is a liquid, debt is a swamp, the world is a stage and hope is a bird:

> 'If I may so express it, I was steeped in Dora. I was not merely over head and ears in love with her, but I was saturated through and through. Enough love might have been wrung out of me, metaphorically speaking, to drown anybody in; and yet there would have remained enough within me, and all over me, to pervade my entire existence.'
> Dickens, *David Copperfield*

> 'Lydgate was in debt... he was every day getting deeper into that swamp, which tempts men towards it with such a pretty covering of flowers and verdure. It is wonderful how soon a man gets up to his chin there.'
> Eliot, *Middlemarch*

> 'All the world's a stage,
> And all the men and women merely players;
> They have their exits and their entrances;
> And one man in his time plays many parts,
> His acts being seven ages.'
> Shakespeare, *As You Like It*

> Hope is the thing with feathers
> That perches in the soul.
> And sings the tune without the words -
> And never stops - at all -
> Dickinson, *"Hope" is the Thing with Feathers*

Extended metaphor can also be presented in stages. In *Bleak House*, Dickens describes a young urchin, Jo, clinging on to life like a draught animal struggling to pull a cart. The metaphor is established:

> 'To Mr Jarndyce, Jo repeats in substance what he said in the morning; without any material variation. Only that cart of his is heavier to draw, and draws with a hollower sound.'

After several pages, the boy worsens and the metaphor is revisited:

> 'For the cart so hard to draw is near its journey's end, and drags over stony ground.'

And again:

> 'The cart had nearly given up, but labours on a little more.'

Until he is about to die:

> 'The cart is shaken all to pieces, and the rugged road is very near its end.'
> Dickens, *Bleak House*

Figures of Association

Metonymy, Synecdoche, Merism, Antonomasia

METONYMY
(Meh TOH ni mi)
Representation by association

Whereas metaphor creates similitude by transposing unrelated things from diverse conceptual domains, metonymy represents people, objects and ideas with associated things from the same domain. In Edward Bulwer-Lytton's popular adage, 'The pen is mightier than the sword', two metonymies are being used: the pen, associated with writing, represents academic and political argument, and the sword, being a weapon, represents violence and war. In both cases the targets and sources are related by association rather than similitude.

Many metonymies are so common that they go unnoticed: 'Hollywood was celebrating', 'the back-benches are in rebellion', 'a heart attack on a plate'. The literal meanings are nonsensical but they are so common that they are simple to decipher:

Hollywood = residents

Back-benches = politicians

Heart attack = an unhealthy meal

It can also be seen in these idiomatic examples how representation by association can often elevate or demean whatever is being described. Metonymy employs several different types of association, the most popular of which are categorised below:

Types of Metonymy
Place for people
Place for event
Object for user/owner
Job for person
Object for action
Action for object
Action for related action

Place for People:
Metonymy often represents people, groups of people or even nations by the place they reside or work. In a statement like, 'the White House questioned the veracity of the allegations', the building is being substituted for the person or people speaking on behalf of the American president. (It is important to distinguish this type of metonymy from personification: the White House is being given no human attributes; it is only being used to represent the people in charge.)

In *Dubliners,* James Joyce metonymizes some corrupt officials when a character declares, 'I believe half of them are in the pay of the castle'; he uses the castle to represent the authorities who are governing Ireland for the British state. He could have written, 'they are in the pay of the British authorities', but by using 'castle' he gives them an air of strength and perhaps medieval power. In the first of the following examples it is the people of India who have risen against the British Empire:

'The whole country was up like a swarm of bees.'
Doyle, *The Sign of Four*

'When he the ambitious Norway combated.'
Shakespeare, *Hamlet*

'To the great delight of the village.'
Dickens, *Bleak House*

'The whole school rose simultaneously, as if moved by a common spring.'
Brontë, *Jane Eyre*

'The place had also a more abiding effect; it drank hard.'
Hardy, *Tess of the d'Urbervilles*

In Hardy's example, the place represents the hard-drinking inhabitants. A popular present-day place-for-people example is the phrase, 'Save the planet'. Since, even with the worst of intentions, the human race is unlikely to destroy the entire planet, what is being referred to, is the environment and its ability to support life. The phrase is actually saying save the people; the planet itself is quite safe. Unless, of course, there is some huge asteroid hurtling towards us or the sun is expanding. The same confusion could arise if George Harrison's *Here Comes the Sun* was taken literally. Thankfully, he was talking metonymically about sunshine and not predicting armageddon.

Place for Event / Date for Event:
   The name of a place is often used for a significant historical event that occurred in that location. Dunkirk for the British retreat, the Alamo for the battle and defence of the mission and Bannockburn for the Scottish victory. A sub-category of 'place for event' is 'date for event': 1066 is the Norman conquest of England. 1492 is Columbus' arrival in the Americas. When it is said that '9/11 was a new Pearl Harbour' or 'this could be a Watergate moment', the metonymy can not only underline the historical significance of the latest event but also foment national pride or outrage.

Object for user/owner:
   The dehumanising representation of people as objects can demean or empower. Journalists and newspaper publishers are frequently referred to as 'the press', describing them as machinery. If someone informs us that the trains are on strike, we understand that what they actually mean is that the train drivers and railwaymen are taking industrial action. By representing the workers as the trains they drive, they are subtly depersonalised. When a waiter says, 'the double cheeseburger at table two is complaining', any sense of identity is taken away from the customer by referring to him as his order. In the following example, writers are represented as a tool of their trade:

   'Let other pens dwell on guilt and misery.'
   Jane Austen

Job for person:
   Another effective way of reducing the importance of a character is to represent them solely by their job title.

   'He ordered the boots to bring in the gentleman's
   luggage.'
   Dickens, *The Pickwick Papers*

The 'boots' is the lowest ranking servant in the household.

Object for action

Another popular metonymy is the use of an object to represent what it does. Perhaps the most well-known object-for-action example comes from Shakespeare's *Julius Caesar*: 'Friends, Romans, countrymen, lend me your ears'; as the ears are associated with hearing, they are used metonymically as a request to listen.

When someone speaks with uncharacteristic bravado after a few drinks, it is excused as the 'whisky talking'. The behaviour is represented by the thing that made them drunk. In the following examples, objects represent the actions they are used for:

> 'Nothing will end this civil war save the edge of the sword.'
> Scott, *Old Mortality*

> 'To prevent us with a pistol bullet.'
> Stevenson, *The Treasure of Franchard*

> 'Naturally there was no end to his tongue then.'
> Dickens, *Bleak House*

Action for object:

An action can also be used to represent an object: A new pair of shoes may be described as 'some new kicks' or trousers as 'nice strides'.

Action for related action:

Occasionally, one action is used to represent an associated action such as 'boil the kettle' for 'make some tea'. A call to arms and battle is metonymised by Scott in *Old Mortality*: 'A demand which would not have been listened to had it not been accompanied with the sound of the trumpet.' Scott also uses metonymy for execution:

> 'I like nane o' your sermons that end in a psalm in the Grassmarket.' (hanging)
> Scott, *Old Mortality*

> 'He'll turn his wee finger to the ceiling oftener than he puts his forefinger to the pen.' (drink/ write)
> Brown, *The House with the Green Shutters*

In this example, Brown presents two metonymies of action. One represents drinking and the other university work.

Synecdoche, Merism and Antonomasia are occasionally grouped under metonymy. However, as they are such important and distinct figures, they each have individual entries in this guide. (see also the short differentiation following synecdoche.)

SYNECDOCHE
(si NEK doh keh)
Part for whole or whole for part

Synecdoche is a trope in which a part of something is used to represent the whole or the whole to represent a part. Unlike metonymy which uses association between target and source, in synecdoche, the source is physically part of the target or vice versa. When someone talks of 'a hundred head of cattle' or 'the police at the door' they do not mean detached heads or the entire police force. These are the two main types of synecdoche: Part-for-Whole and Whole-for-Part.

Part for Whole Synecdoche
The most common form of synecdoche is part-for-whole. In the naval command, 'all hands on deck', hands are used to represent the sailors and if someone buys 'a new set of wheels' they have most likely purchased a car or bike.

Anatomy for Person:
Synecdoches are quite common when referring to people in everyday speech. If we say we hate 'someone's guts', we mean the actual person rather than just the stomach or entrails, and if a football manager sends a 'fresh pair of legs' onto the field, it means an entire player. Various parts of the body are used to represent the whole person:

'Take thy face hence.'
Shakespeare, *Macbeth*

'It doth not become a young head to instruct grey hairs.'
Scott, *Heart of Midlothian*

> 'A dinner which would have been cheap at half-a-crown a mouth.'
> Dickens, *The Pickwick Papers*

> 'I don't let her put her foot in here.'
> Stevenson, *The Beach of Falesá*

> 'Guppy becomes conscious of a manly whisker emerging from the cloistered walk below.'
> Dickens, *Bleak House*

> 'The young culprit got some of the best blood of the land to enter as his securities, and was set at liberty.'
> Hogg, *Confessions of a Justified Sinner*

Attire for Person:
Presenting someone as what they are wearing can be employed critically, sarcastically or simply to reduce them to the status of a stock character. A businessman is often referred to as a 'suit' and a manual worker as a 'hard hat'. In *Bleak House*, after a fire, Dickens simply describes a fireman by saying, 'One helmet remains behind'. In this case, he uses the figure ingenuously to describe a character unimportant to the plot. However, synecdoche can also have an intentionally reductive effect. In the following example, a young would-be stenographer who has just been rejected, is described as her ostentatious silver-heart pendant:

> 'The silver heart left the office, swinging and banging itself independently against the office furniture as it indignantly departed.'
> O Henry, *The Romance of a Busy Broker*

> 'The boots were approaching again.'
> Orwell, *Nineteen Eighty-Four*

> 'I'll begin with that sulky blue-bonnet in the ingle-nook.'
> Scott, *Old Mortality*

> 'Doublet and hose ought to show itself courageous to petticoat.'
> Shakespeare, *As You Like It*

Dickens uses this same type of synecdoche to instil a little mystery when a character first appears in a scene:

'A grey cloak and umbrella, unknown to Chesney Wold at other periods, are seen among the leaves.'
Dickens, *Bleak House*

'On the box of which vehicle a very tall hat makes itself manifest to the public.'
Dickens, *Bleak House*

Other Part-for-Whole examples

Material:
Often an object is represented as the material from which it is made. We say we are 'using plastic to pay' rather than credit card or refer to clothes as 'threads'.

'I gave him the cold steel for all I was worth.'
Stevenson, *The Beach of Falesá*

Architecture:

'I had left a hostile roof with a desperate and embittered heart.'
Brontë, *Jane Eyre*

Time:

'Cold in the earth - and fifteen wild Decembers.'
Brontë, *Cold in th' Earth*

Political Geography:

England for UK. Britain for UK. Holland for Netherlands. Russia for Soviet Union.

Whole for Part Synecdoche

Political geography is also used in whole-for-part synecdoche as when quite often people use 'America' when they are referring only to the United States. In the first of the following examples, an ill child is described as the entire disease:

'Here is the fever coming up the street.'
Dickens, *Bleak House*

'Pour down thy weather.'
Shakespeare, *King John*

'The police said that he was walking home in the dark when he fell down a hill.'
Doyle, *The Five Orange Pips*

Container for Contents:
A container often represents whatever it contains. Working for your pay-packet does not mean just the envelope. No one is confused when a 'dish' is used to refer to the food it holds, a friend may ask if you would like 'a glass' rather than 'some wine' and if someone invites you to 'bring a bottle', they will be surprised if you arrive with an empty one.

'And still I can join in a cup and a song.'
Burns, *Jolly Beggars*

But a club of good fellows, like those that are here,
And a bottle like this, are my glory and care.
Burns, *No Churchman am I*

Synecdoche / Metonymy

Synecdoche is often described as a special case of metonymy and it would be difficult to argue that being part of something is not a kind of association. There is also some debate as to whether Container-for-Contents is truly Whole-for-Part. Nonetheless, in certain cases, there are distinct differences between the two figures. These can be exemplified by comparing how each trope treats similar things. Synecdoche would use 'nice wheels' to describe a car, whereas a metonymy would be 'nice ride'. Similarly, if a policeman is at the door, synecdoche would describe him as 'the police' whereas metonymy would use 'the law'. Even the same word in different contexts can be used by both figures. The 'crown', synecdochically represents the monarch when being worn, but when used to represent political power it is metonymy. 'Boots' when naming the boy who cleans boots in a hotel, is metonymy but 'boots on the ground' is synecdoche. Another military example, 'redcoats' can also be employed by both figures. In *Bleak House*, Dickens' ex-soldier announces, 'I have done with the red coat, believe me'; this is metonymy as it represents the army by association. However, in a famous quote by Louisa May Alcott, she complains, 'Poor dull Concord. Nothing colorful has come through here since the redcoats'; Alcott's redcoats are synecdoches as they are part of the soldiers' uniforms. Likewise, in the popular synecdoche 'all hands on deck', hands are sailors, but in the metonymy 'I need a hand', the hand is merely associated with help. Therefore, the figures have a close relationship but also distinct uses.

Finally, here is an example of both synecdoche and metonymy being used in conjunction to represent the same child:

'Howling to the sky for the loss of thirty pounds of freckles and mischief.'
    O Henry, *Between Rounds*

MERISM
(ME riz m)
Parts or extremes represent all

Whereas synecdoche can represent the whole of something by using one part, merism uses several parts or two extremes. Examples can be found in everyday speech: 'from dawn till dusk', 'part and parcel', 'day in and day out'. In many idiomatic merisms, the initial literal meaning is practically forgotten and they now simply represent the generality of 'all'. This can be seen in the expression 'lock, stock and barrel', originally from the parts of a gun or 'hook, line and sinker', from fishing equipment. Merism is often employed in official ceremonies and vows. In many weddings, rather than simply promising to love each other forever, the couple swear to a wide range of merisms: 'For better, for worse, for richer, for poorer, in sickness and in health'. When honouring the war dead, we promise to remember them 'at the going down of the sun and in the morning'. A master of ceremonies, rather than speaking to 'everyone', will most likely address the crowd as 'ladies and gentlemen, boys and girls'.

There are two different types of merism - parts and extremes:

Merism of Parts

A target can be split into important, significant or simply colourful parts: The body is composed of 'flesh and bone', searching everywhere would include 'every nook and cranny' and the phrase, 'rag, tag and bobtail' originally represented the common rabble.

> 'By earth, sea and sky, thou dost me injustice!'
> Scott, *Ivanhoe*

> 'O'er fields and towns from sea to sea'
> Shelley, *The Mask of Anarchy*

> 'Being able to turn me out of this place, neck and crop.'
> Dickens, *Bleak House*

> 'He has passed all his life on board a vessel, and has scarcely and idea beyond rope and shroud.'
> Shelley, *Frankenstein*

Merism of Extremes

Merism can also use polar extremes or opposites to represent the entirety of what comes between: 'from the cradle to the grave' represents an entire life; when looking for something people will 'search high and low' and perhaps struggle 'through thick and thin'.

> 'From creation to decay.'
> Shelley, *Hellas*

> 'The power we have to fight for night and day.'
> Orwell, *Nineteen Eighty-Four*

> 'From the soles of thy feet to the crown of thy head, there is nothing interesting about thee.'
> Dickens, *Bleak House*

> 'Making arrangements for moving heaven and earth.'
> Dickens, *Bleak House*

Entirety Included

Another useful technique is to present the target in its entirety before the merism:

'I lov'd thee, and show'd thee all the qualities o' th' isle,
the fresh springs, brine-pits, barren place and fertile.'
Shakespeare, *The Tempest*

'By every means, legal or illegal.'
Scott, *Ivanhoe*

Subjects of Merism

Throughout literature there are countless examples of subjects being represented meristically:

Merism of Body:

'I do not see hide or hair of anyone there.'
Runyon, *The Melancholy Dane*

'I'll go at it tooth and nail.'
Dickens, *David Copperfield*

'Fire to come down from heaven, I suppose, and consume me bones and baggage.'
Stevenson, *The Beach of Falesá*

'The devil's agents may be of flesh and blood, may they not?'
Doyle, *The Hound of the Baskervilles*

Merism of Attire:

'Minutely inspecting that gentleman's appearance, from the crown of his hat to the lowest button of his gaiters.'
Dickens, *The Pickwick Papers*

Merism of Household:

'Have even made it known in the house itself: upstairs, downstairs, and in my lady's chamber.'
Dickens, *Bleak House*

'Jennet Clouston has called down the curse on him and his house, byre and stable, man, guest, and master, wife, miss or bairn.'
Stevenson, *Kidnapped*

Merism of Place:

'He knows each glade and dingle, copse and high-wood.'
Scott, *Ivanhoe*

'The palace, the night-cellar, the jail, the madhouse: the chambers of birth and death, of health and sickness... midnight was upon them all.'
Dickens, *Oliver Twist*

Merism of Time:

'The woman's unceasing and unwearied exertions, early and late, morning, noon, and night, kept them above actual want.'
Dickens, *The Pickwick Papers*

'I was termed naughty and tiresome, sullen and sneaking, from morning to noon, and from noon to night.'
Brontë, *Jane Eyre*

'Weeks, months, seasons, pass along.'
Dickens, *David Copperfield*

'On he wandered, night and day: beneath the blazing sun, and the cold pale moon: through the dry heat of noon, and the damp cold of night: in the grey light of morn, and the red glare of eve.'
Dickens, *The Pickwick Papers* *(Prince Bladud)*

Merism of People:

'Be he plaintiff or be he defendant, be his name Pickwick, or Noakes, or Stoakes, or Stiles, or Brown or Thompson.'
Dickens, *The Pickwick Papers*

'Sent them to hell by the slump, tag, rag, and bobtail!'
Hogg, *Confessions of a Justified Sinner*

'All the writers of the age, good, bad, and indifferent.'
Smollett, *The Expedition of Humphry Clinker*

Merism of Activity:

'The noise of carriages and carts, the rattle of wheels, the cries of men and boys, all the busy sounds of the mighty multitude instinct with life and occupation, blended into one deep murmur, floated into the room.'
Dickens, *The Pickwick Papers*

'He is a well-known character around Broadway, because he is always in and out, and up and down, and around and about.'
Runyon, *So You Won't Talk*

Multiple Merisms:

'I will serve you on my bended knees, by night and by day, by land and by water.'
Smollett, *The Expedition of Humphry Clinker*

'They all went down into the dining-room, where it was full of tag, rag, and bobtail, dancing, singing, and drinking.'
Pepys, *Diary*

'They're [his horses] wittles and drink to me - lodging, wife, and children - reading, writing, and arithmetic - snuff, tobacker, and sleep.'
Dickens, *David Copperfield*

ANTONOMASIA
(An toh noh MAZE ee ah)
Epithet for proper name or name for quality

Antonomasia is derived from the Greek for 'different name' and has two main forms which almost mirror one another. The first substitutes a well-known epithet for a proper name and the second uses a famous proper name to for its associated qualities.

Epithet for Name

The first form of antonomasia includes nicknames or epithets for famous characters: the 'Little Corporal' for Napoleon, the 'Red

Baron' for Manfred Von Richthofen, 'Satchmo' for Louis Armstrong and the 'Man of Steel' for either Superman or Stalin. It is also used for famous places: 'the Big Apple' for New York, 'the Windy City' for Chicago and 'Auld Reekie' for Edinburgh. Antonomasia is used as a kind of shorthand to present recognisable characters or things:

> 'Rats, weevils, and lawyers were created by Old Harry.'
> (the devil)
>> Eliot, *The Mill on the Floss*

> O thou, whatever title suits thee!
> Auld Hornie, Satan, Nick, or Clootie.
>> Burns, *Address to the Deil*

> 'Inspiring bold John Barleycorn.' (whisky)
>> Burns, *Tam O'Shanter*

Name for Quality

The second form of antonomasia uses a famous name to transfer the associated qualities. These can be positive as in 'he is an Einstein' or 'a Romeo' or negative, as in 'a Quisling' or 'a Judas'.

> 'Ex-Professor Moriarty of mathematical celebrity…is the Napoleon of crime, Watson.'
>> Doyle, *The Final Problem*

> 'I told you she was a Johnny Bull.' (English ship)
>> Stevenson, *The Wrecker*

> 'He was a perfect Whittington, without his cat, or the remotest chance of becoming Lord Mayor.'
>> Dickens, *David Copperfield*

> 'I let him run on, this papier-mâché Mephistopheles.'
>> Conrad, *Heart of Darkness*

> 'How are you, my Bacchanal?'
>> Dickens, *David Copperfield*

> 'A large man with a Quixotic nose.'
>> Stevenson, *The Treasure of Franchard*

Epitheton

Another figure worthy of mention is 'epitheton'. This device produces antonomasia when an adjective is added to a famous name which then, through time and usage, becomes an indispensable part. For example: 'Fierce Achilles', 'Wise Nestor', 'Mighty Zeus', 'Perfidious Albion', 'Bonnie Prince Charlie' and 'Bloody Mary'. These examples are antonomasias as they include the target names.

However, epitheton is also used in less particular situations outwith antonomasia in adjective-noun pairings such as 'unbridled passion', 'filthy lucre' and 'diamond geezer'.

Figures of Exaggeration

Hyperbole, Metalepsis, Catachresis, Synaesthesia

HYPERBOLE
(Hi PER bo leh)
Emphasis by exaggeration

Hyperbole is the all-encompassing figurative term for exaggeration. It is often found in advertising such as 'out of this world' or 'a once in a lifetime offer' and in everyday speech: 'I've told you a million times', 'I'd give my right arm' or 'the suitcase weighed a ton'. Hyperbole is used widely in literature to express strong emotions like the eternal nature of love in Burns' *Red Red Rose*: 'Till a' the seas gang dry my dear and rocks melt wi' the sun.' Many different subjects are targeted with hyperbole:

Hyperbole of Magnitude

Size is a common target for exaggeration. In the following example, the corpulent Falstaff is the target:

> 'This sanguine coward, this bed-presser, this horseback-breaker, this huge hill of flesh.'
> Shakespeare, *Henry IV*

> 'She has a face the size of a town clock and enough chins for a fire escape.'
> Runyon, *A Piece of Pie*

Hyperbole of Smallness

Hyperbole need not always be incremental. Exaggeration also works diminutively:

> 'He could see Mr. Claypole taking cold beef from the dish, and porter from the pot, and administering homeopathic doses of both to Charlotte.'
> Dickens, *Oliver Twist*

> 'A little Judy with as much bathing suit as will make a boxing glove for a mosquito.'
> Runyon, *A Job for the Macarone*

The Metaphoric Manual

Hyperbole of Number:

'Scarce one but possessed fifty times his weight of brain.'
    Brown, *The House with the Green Shutters*

'A thousand times I would have shed my blood, drop by drop, to have saved their lives.'
    Shelley, *Frankenstein*

'He hath borne me on his back a thousand times.'
    Shakespeare, *Hamlet*

'Let Faustus live in hell a thousand years, a hundred thousand, and at last be sav'd!'
    Marlowe, *Doctor Faustus*

'I have full cause of weeping; but this heart shall break into a hundred thousand flaws, or ere I'll weep.'
    Shakespeare, *King Lear*

'To blaze your marriage, reconcile your friends,
Beg pardon of the prince, and call thee back
With twenty hundred thousand times more joy
Than thou went'st forth in lamentation.'
    Shakespeare, *Romeo and Juliet*

Hyperbole of Time:

'During the three terrible hours that the play had lasted, he had lived centuries of pain, aeon upon aeon of torture.'
    Wilde, *The Picture of Dorian Gray*

'The speed of lightning was slow to the wishes of revenge.'
    Galt, *Ringan Gilhaizie*

Other examples

    Hyperbole is in no way restricted to the preceding themes. Apparently, the sky is not the limit when it comes to this figure:

"What's he like?" / "I've been dying to tell you."
  James, *The Turn of the Screw*

'It gave him a weirdly voracious aspect, as though he had wanted to swallow all the air, all the earth, all the men before him.'
  Conrad, *Heart of Darkness*

'Not all the rain that ever fell or ever will fall, will put as much of hell's fire out, as a man can carry about with him.'
  Dickens, *Oliver Twist*

'The whole town so clean you might have dined upon the causeway.'
  Stevenson, *Catriona*

'She wants eight gallons of his heart's blood and both legs in the divorce settlement.'
  Runyon, *Broadway Incident*

'If anybody had dropped a postage-stamp in Brodick that day, it would have sounded like a dynamite explosion.'
  Munro, *The Vital Spark*

'There could not have been more ink about [In the office], if it had been roofless from its first construction, and the skies had rained, snowed, hailed and blown ink through the varying seasons of the year.'
  Dickens, *David Copperfield*

CATACHRESIS
(Kat ah KREE sis)
Over-exaggerated metaphor

Catachresis is a trope in which figures are presented is such a way that they appear confusing or erroneous. The names derives from the Greek for abuse and was originally reserved to describe semantic errors. There are now two figurative types: The first, when the device is so complex that it is difficult to decipher and the second, also known as 'mixed metaphor', when an idiomatic phrase is presented incorrectly.

Complex Catachresis

On occasion, words are brought together that seem to defy interpretation or appear to be erroneous in grammar or logic. These complex catachreses can employ a variety of other figures such as simile, metaphor and anthimeria:

> 'I lent my love to losse and gaged my life in vaine.'
> Puttenham, *The Arte of English Poesie*

> Arsenic fish like sharks,
> Sharks like wailing drops that blind the crowd.
> Lorca, *Cry to Rome*

One of the most famous lines in theatre would have been catachrestic at the time, but because of its popularity, has lost the initial shock value and has become commonly understood:

> 'I will speak daggers to her, but use none.' (also anthimeria)
> Shakespeare, *Hamlet*

Mixed Metaphor

The over-use of certain metaphors and idioms can lead to them being combined in error. On occasion the results are ridiculous and sometimes comic: 'the manager had a fresh pair of legs up his sleeve', 'killing two birds with one bush', 'beating about the bush with the wrong end of the stick', 'throwing a spanner amongst the pigeons'. This type of catachresis often occurs in broadcasting where, because of the pressure of live sports and rolling news, many unintentional mixed metaphors are produced. A recent interviewee on live news combined the popular political metaphors, 'milking the system' and 'having their snouts in the trough' to produce 'politicians milking the trough.' One eighteenth-century politician, Boyle Roche, was well known for creating mixed metaphors such as: 'Mr Speaker, I smell a rat; I see him forming in the air and darkening the sky; but I'll nip him in the bud.'

METALEPSIS
(Meh ta LEP sis)
Tropes multiplied or effect from remote cause

Sometimes described as an exaggerated kind of metonymy, metalepsis is perhaps the most difficult of all the tropes to decipher. Puttenham refers to it as 'farset' or 'far-fetched' and notes the 'hearer's conceit strangely entangled by the figure'. There are two main figurative types of metalepsis: layering of devices and the attribution of effect to a remote cause.

Layered Devices

Many figures can be combined for effect, such as, hyperbolic simile or euphemistic metaphor. However, metalepsis, rather than combining figures, uses one figure as a platform for another whilst leaving the initial figure unspoken. For example, if someone is described as using 'culinary' arguments, it can be deciphered thus: 'culinary' is a metonym for 'kitchen equipment', as in pot and kettle, and 'the pot calling the kettle black' is a popular metaphor for hypocrisy. Therefore a 'culinary' argument would mean a 'hypocritical' argument. These are simple when explained but can often be like cryptic crossword clues. Consequently, as with catachresis, there is an element of subjectivity regarding the audience's prior knowledge of the tropes being layered.

'The long divorce of steel falls on me.'
Shakespeare, *Henry VIII*

'Succeeded by certain arguments, metallic or otherwise.'
Doyle, *The Copper Beeches*

'I will love thee still, my dear, /While the sands o' life shall run.'
Burns, *Red, Red Rose*

Remote Cause

Metalepsis is also the term used when a target is linked to a remote cause. A popular example is found when Medea's degree of sorrow is compared in size to a mountain; specifically the mountain on which the tree that became the mast of the ship that brought Jason to start her troubles had grown:

Woe worth the mountain that the mast bare
Which was the first cause of all my care.
   Euripedes, *Medea*

'We still have the Forth to pass, Davie - weary fall the rains that fed and the hillsides that guided it!'
   Stevenson, *Kidnapped*

'Honour to the soil that grew the grape, to the grape that made the wine, to the sun that ripened it, and to the merchant who adulterated it!'
   Dickens, *David Copperfield*

'Was this the face that launched a thousand ships and burnt the topless towers of Ilium?'
   Marlowe, *Doctor Faustus*

SYNAESTHESIA
(Sin as THEEZ ya)
Mixing senses

Synaesthesia, in figurative terms, is a sensory exaggeration. This may entail hearing colours or seeing sounds. Quite common in everyday speech: 'he has a terrible taste in music', 'wearing a loud shirt', 'a voice like velvet'. (Amongst literary devices it also has the peculiarity of being an actual neurological condition and is described medically as a 'merging of senses'.) Any combination of senses is possible and some are visited frequently, but others could prove to be rather challenging. The following examples are a selection of the most popular synaesthetic combinations:

Tasting Sound:

'As if the words were something real in his mouth and delicious to taste.'
   Dickens, *David Copperfield*

'Some cried ; some swore; and the tropes and figures of Billingsgate were used without reserve in all their native zest and flavour.'
   Smollett, *The Expedition of Humphry Clinker*

'The sweet tones of her voice, and the softness of her reply.'
   Scott, *Ivanhoe*

Tasting Sight:

'Tasting of Flora and the country green, Dance, and Provencal song, and sun burnt mirth!'
   Keats, *Ode to a Nightingale*

The light tastes like worn out metal
   Lorca, *Moon and Panorama of the Insects*

Hearing Sight:

'They wore noisy dresses.'
   Joyce, *Dubliners*

Feeling smell:

'The smell hit you on the face with a smack.'
   Orwell, *The Road to Wigan Pier*

'He pushed open the door and a hideous cheesy smell of sour beer hit him in the face.'
   Orwell, *Nineteen Eighty-Four*

Figures of Personification
Personification, Hypostatisation, Anthropomorphism, Zoomorphism

PERSONIFICATION
(Per SON if ih KAY shon)
Human qualities for inanimate things

Personification is a trope in which human or animal qualities or characteristics are attributed to inanimate things like weather, nature and machinery: 'the sun smiled upon us', 'the old tree groaned in the angry wind', 'the brakes screeched in protest'. It is also used in everyday speech such as 'a cruel disease' or 'nasty weather'.

In a wider sense, personification can be an umbrella figure for anything non-human that is given human characteristics. However, there are more precise terms:

Personification	emotional qualities to	non-living things
Hypostatization	human qualities to	abstractions
Anthropomorphism	human qualities to	creatures
Zoomorphism	creature qualities to	humans

Pathetic Fallacy

One of the best known personifications in English poetry is in Wordsworth's *Daffodils* when he declares 'I wandered lonely as a cloud'; of course, clouds can never be lonely, but Wordsworth personifies the cloud in his simile to enhance his own feelings. When the emotions of a character are projected on the surroundings it is known as 'pathetic fallacy'. This, initially derogatory phrase, was coined by John Ruskin in the nineteenth century in protest against what he regarded as exaggerated corruptions of truth in art. However, the phrase is now not at all disparaging and simply used to denote personification.

Countless subjects are targeted with personification and weather is one of the most popular. Shelley employs the figure to such a degree that his entire poem is narrated by the cloud itself:

Personification of Weather:

> I wield the flail of the lashing hail,
> And whiten the green plains under,
> And then again I dissolve it in rain,
> And laugh as I pass in thunder.
> Shelley, *The Cloud*

> The rain set in early tonight
> The sullen wind was soon awake
> It tore the elm tops down for spite
> And did its worst to vex the lake.
> Browning, *Porphyria's Lover*

> 'The day dawneth in the east, and the shadows flee away before it; the winds have gone to their chambers to sleep.'
> Hogg, *The Three Perils of Man*

> 'I heard the thunder hoarsely laugh.'
> Shelley, *Prometheus Unbound*

> 'He was only awakened by the morning sun darting his bright beams reproachfully into the apartment.'
> Dickens, *The Pickwick Papers*

> 'The storm grew louder and louder and the wind cried and sobbed like a child in the chimney.'
> Doyle, *The Five Orange Pips*

Personification of Astronomical Objects:

> 'The murdered man, the blanketed corpse, the lidless coffin, and the open grave, were under no inspection but the moon's.'
> Twain, *Tom Sawyer*

> 'The sun and the heavens, who have viewed my operations, can bear witness of the truth.'
> Shelley, *Frankenstein*

'The declining sun, struggling through the mist which had obscured it all day, looked brightly down upon the little Wiltshire village.'
Dickens, *Martin Chuzzlewit*

'The cold stars shone in mockery.'
Shelley, *Frankenstein*

'The wild moon seemed to plunge headlong, as if, in a dread disturbance of the laws of nature, she had lost her way and were frightened.'
Dickens, *David Copperfield*

Personification of Darkness and Light:

With storms around and fears before
And no kind light to point the shore.
Brontë, *Lines*

'By th'clock 'tis day
And yet dark night strangles the travelling lamp
Is't night's predominance, or the day's shame,
That darkness does the face of earth entomb
When living light should kiss it?'
Shakespeare, *Macbeth*

Personification of Land and Sea:

'They rowed her in across the rolling foam/ The cruel crawling foam/ The cruel hungry foam.'
Kingsley, *The Sands of Dee*

'A wide plain where the broadening Floss hurries on between its green banks to the sea, and the loving tide, rushing to meet it, checks its passage with an impetuous embrace.'
Eliot, *The Mill on the Floss*

See the mountains kiss high Heaven
And the waves clasp one another.
Shelley, *Love's Philosophy*

Personification of Architecture:

'It [the barn] seems to have been hemmed in by the houses round, while dozing, so that it could not escape with the fields feeing from the town.'
   Brown, *The House with the Green Shutters*

'He... threw himself against the thick wall as if to force a passage through the stone; but the strong building mocked his feeble efforts.'
   Dickens, *The Pickwick Papers*

'Each close vomited out its levies.'
   Hogg, *Confessions of a Justified Sinner*

'The brick seemed to be blushing in the walls, and the slates on the roof to have turned pale with shame.'
   Stevenson, *The Wrecker*

'The old chimney quivered with the shock, but stood it bravely.'
   Dickens, *Oliver Twist*

Personification of Furnishings:

'The guests were seated at a table which groaned under the quantity of good cheer.'
   Scott, *Ivanhoe*

'A large badly-furnished apartment, with a dirty grate, in which a small fire was making a wretched attempt to be cheerful.'
   Dickens, *The Pickwick Papers*

'It [The travellers' room] is the right hand parlour, into which an aspiring kitchen fire-place appears to have walked, accompanied by a rebellious poker, tongs and shovel.'
   Dickens, *The Pickwick Papers*

Personification of Plants and Trees:

'Every leaf speaks bliss to me, fluttering from the autumn tree.'
Brontë, *Fall Leaves Fall*

'The dark-faced and pensive forest.'
Conrad, H*eart of Darkness*

'A sunken alley where a few stallkeepers were selling tired-looking vegetables.'
Orwell, *Nineteen-Eighty Four*

Personification of the Grave:

'He had always known that the grave was there and waiting for him.'
Orwell, *Nineteen-Eighty Four*

Personification of Alcohol:

'He pours a radiant nectar, two score and ten years old, that blushes in the glass to find itself so famous.'
Dickens, *Bleak House*

Anti-personification

Occasionally an author may highlight the lack of human qualities to emphasise the true apathy of nature:

'He hoped she would be happy, and never regret having driven her poor boy out into the unfeeling world to suffer and die.'
Twain, *Tom Sawyer*

False personifications:

What may seem, at first glance, examples of personification can in fact prove to be different figures altogether. The most common of these is when metonymy is used to represent people as their locations: 'Downing Street was confused,' is merely a representation of the Prime Minister or government staff; the actual street is not being given human qualities. Hypallage is slightly more difficult to differentiate. Also known as transferred epithet, hypallage shifts a word to an unusual place in the sentence: 'The manager offered an obsequious glass of champagne'; this is a scheme that rearranges the words rather than a trope that personifies the glass. (see metonymy, hypallage)

ANTHROPOMORPHISM
(An thro po MORPH izim)
Human qualities for animals

Anthropomorphism describes human characteristics being given to non-human creatures such as animals, insects and birds. It is often sustained throughout texts such as fables, allowing the characters not only to display human emotions but actually become human in actions, conversation, culture and attire. The figure can be found in short sequences but it is quite common for a creature's human behaviour to continue throughout the entire work:

'The Rabbit actually took a watch out its waistcoat pocket, and looked at it, and then hurried on.'
Carroll, *Alice's Adventures in Wonderland*

'And I am only a black panther. But I love thee, Little Brother.'
Kipling, *The Jungle Book*

'There were only four dissentients, the three dogs and the cat, who was afterwards discovered to have voted on both sides.'
Orwell, *Animal Farm*

ZOOMORPHISM
(Zoo MORPH izim)
Animal qualities for humans

Zoomorphism is a figure in which humans are described as creatures or even gifted with a kind of Darwinian regression in order to bark, howl and slither around: 'the girl purred', 'the teacher growled'. It is prevalent throughout fokelore and religion where gods and mythological characters would often take animal or semi-animal form. Zoomorphism is also used ubiquitously in comics and movies to create superheroes who require animal or insect abilities in their crime fighting adventures. In literature, characters are frequently presented as non-human:

> 'And he meets you again, at half-past nine, and greets you as a serpent.'
> Dickens, *The Pickwick Papers*

> 'Some of those evil persons, who, for hire or malice, had made themselves the beagles of the persecutors.'
> Galt, *Ringan Gilhaizie*

> 'An election is coming. Universal peace is declared, and the foxes have a sincere interest in prolonging the lives of the poultry.'
> Eliot, *Felix Holt*

> 'The hideous old man seemed like some loathsome reptile, engendered in the slime and darkness through which he moved.'
> Dickens, *Oliver Twist*

> 'The company and the sixpences for tea, poured in, in shoals.'
> Dickens, *The Pickwick Papers*

> 'The telescreen barked at him.'
> Orwell, *Nineteen Eighty-Four*

> 'Herrick had now spat his venom.'
> Stevenson, *The Ebb Tide*

This trope has a much darker side when it is used for creeds or races. Real controversy arose recently when the British Prime Minister chose the same word to refer to desperate migrants and refugees: 'You have got a swarm of people coming across the Mediterranean.' (*ITV News 2016*)

HYPOSTATIZATION
(HI po stat eye ZAY shon)
Human qualities for abstractions

Hypostatization is a type of personification that deals with abstractions such as time, love and guilt: 'Time is against us', 'Love will find a way', 'Guilt suffocates me every day'. Emotion and volition are attributed to a wide variety of non-living, intangible ideas. Although in most cases the qualities being transferred are human, on occasion, the abstractions are brought to life as creatures or monsters. (The target words are often capitalised, but although helpful to the reader, this is not a strict rule.)

A wide variety of abstractions are targeted:

'Fate seemed to be playing a series of extraordinarily unamusing jokes.'
Orwell, *Down and Out in Paris and London*

'We drove through drifts of rotting vegetation - sad gifts, as it seemed to me, for Nature to throw before the carriage of the returning heir of the Baskervilles.'
Doyle, *The Hound of the Baskervilles*

'Great Nature spoke to me; and soothed me to lay down my weary head upon the grass.'
Dickens, *David Copperfield*

'Time will, perhaps, furnish occasion.'
Smollett, *The Expedition of Humphry Clinker*

'I hope Time will be good to you.'
Dickens, *David Copperfield*

'Patience has sat upon it a long time.'
Dickens, *Bleak House*

'The fangs of remorse tore my bosom.'
Shelley, *Frankenstein*

'She had no companions but silence and loneliness.'
Twain, *Tom Sawyer*

The Gender of Hypostatization

Targets of hypostatization are frequently attributed a gender, usually female, sometimes male and occasionally presented as 'it':

Female Hypostatization:

> Hope, whose whisper would have given
> Balm to all my frenzied pain,
> Stretched her wings, and soared to heaven,
> Went, and ne'er returned again!
> Brontë, *Hope*

> 'Reason had long been tottering on her throne.'
> Hogg, *The Three Perils of Man*

> 'Nature walked on bank and brae, in maiden pride, spreading and showing her flowery mantle to the sun.'
> Galt, *Ringan Gilhaizie*

> 'As if Nature herself had tried to ward off intruders.'
> Conrad, *Heart of Darkness*

> 'Vice… takes up her abode in many temples.'
> Dickens, *Oliver Twist*

> 'Love, as usual in such cases, borrowed the name of friendship, used her language, and claimed her privileges.'
> Scott, *Old Mortality*

> 'The event of the day had passed and vacancy resumed her reign.'
> Brown, *The House with the Green Shutters*

Male Hypostatization:

> I met Murder on the way
> He had a mask like Castlereagh.
> Shelley, *The Mask of Anarchy*

'Like a couple of sentinels long forgotten on their post by
the Black Serjeant, Death.'
Dickens, *Bleak House*

Of course, the serjeant (sic) could be female, but perhaps the less palatable abstractions are reserved for masculinity. In the following poem, John Keats includes several examples. Disappointment is feminine, Despair is masculine and Hope has the epithet, 'sweet':

Should Disappointment, parent of Despair,
Strive for her son to seize my careless heart;
When, like a cloud, he sits upon the air,
Preparing on his spell-bound prey to dart:
Chase him away, sweet Hope, with visage bright,
And fright him as the morning frightens night!
Keats, *To Hope*

Non-Human Hypostatization

In an immortal line from *Othello*, Shakespeare opts for the non-human:

'O beware, my lord, of jealousy; It is the green-eyed monster which doth mock the meat it feeds on.'
Shakespeare, *Othello*

In a similar vein, James Hogg creates a multi-tasking evil spirit:

'It was evident that the demon of animosity and revenge was now conjured up'
Hogg, *The Three Perils of Man*

Multiple Hypostatization

As in Hogg's example above, quite often an author will present more than one hypostatization at a time:

'Profligacy and riot have staggered home to dream.'
Dickens, *Oliver Twist*

'Envy always dogs Merit at the heels.'
Scott, *Old Mortality*

> 'A shameful testimony to the future ages, how civilisation and barbarism walked this boastful island together.'
> Dickens, *Bleak House*

> 'When Vice quits the stage for a moment, her place is immediately occupied by Folly.'
> Smollett, *The Expedition of Humphry Clinker*

However, glory smiles upon Charles Dickens for using four together:

> 'Ignominy, Want, Despair, and Madness, have collectively or separately, been the attendants of my career.'
> Dickens, *David Copperfield*

Apostrophe

Apostrophe is a device which is often linked to hypostatisation. It refers to a character or narrator turning in mid sentence to address an abstraction, a deity, a dead person or indeed anyone or thing that is not actually present. Rather than a trope, it is more of a scheme or a term of rhetoric. (see anacoluthon) It can, however, occasionally employ hypostatization, therefore, a few examples are included here for clarity:

> 'Because I know, or believe, Mr. Rochester is living: and then, to die of want and cold is a fate to which nature cannot submit passively. Oh, Providence! sustain me a little longer! Aid!—direct me!'
> Brontë, *Jane Eyre*

> 'Why, she's a liar to the end! Where is she? Not there—not in heaven—not perished—where? Oh! you said you cared nothing for my sufferings! And I pray one prayer—I repeat it till my tongue stiffens—Catherine Earnshaw, may you not rest as long as I am living; you said I killed you—haunt me, then!'
> Brontë, *Wuthering Heights*

'He whom it would relieve, nor eats nor hungers any more…on errands of life, these letters speed to death. Ah, Bartleby! Ah, humanity!'
    Melville, *Bartleby, the Scrivener*

'Am I to lose all, without a chance of retrieval? Is Hareton to be a beggar? Oh, damnation! I will have it back.'
    Brontë, *Wuthering Heights*

Ironies

Literary irony encompasses a wide range of devices which use double meaning or employ opposites. Nonetheless, in many collections of literary terms it is presented as a single device. This overlooks the wide variety of ironic figures; some ironies are closely related to tropes others are have a much closer relationship to schemes. For example, antiphrasis, uses substitution and could be regarded as a trope along with the group of ironic understatements, whereas oxymoron, which juxtaposes opposites, is more akin to a scheme. Furthermore, antithesis and antanaclasis, although primarily achieving their effects through ambiguity, rely on structure and repetition respectively. Therefore, irony is best viewed as a wider group of devices that connect with both tropes and schemes.

Figures of Understatement

Meiosis, Euphemism, Dysphemism, Tapinosis, Litotes

Understatement is often used as a catch-all for a group of reductive figures, however, each has it's own distinct effect: meiosis represents things in a modest sense to bring them into focus, euphemism makes undesirable things sound better and dysphemism primarily makes things worse. Litotes negates an opposite and tapinosis belittles. Examples of these functions are shown in the table where each understates death in a different form of irony:

Understating Death

Meiosis	Taken his last breath
Euphemism	Gone to a better place
Dysphemism	Food for the worms
Tapinosis	One less Xmas present to buy
Litotes	Not the liveliest member of the family

MEIOSIS
(my OH sis)
Understatement for emphasis

Meiosis is a form of understatement in which good or bad things are described modestly but in a way that also ironically focuses attention on the idea. This is exemplified when referring to the Atlantic Ocean as 'the pond' or 'the drink'.

Whereas euphemism softens the tone of a situation, meiosis understates things to highlight them:

> And was wondering if the man had done
> A great or little thing,
> When a voice behind me whispered low,
> 'That fellow's got to swing.' (hang)
> Wilde, *The Ballad Of Reading Gaol*

'I fancy Kurtz felt too ill that day to care, or there would have been mischief.' (bloodshed)
Conrad, *Heart of Darkness*

'These are changed days since your cousin and I heard the balls whistle in our lugs.' (battle)
Stevenson, *Catriona*

'Ay, ay, a scratch, a scratch; Marry, 'tis enough. Where is my page? Go, villain, fetch a surgeon.' (he is mortally wounded)
Shakespeare, *Romeo and Juliet*

'It's a cruel ploy, for it has spilt muckle good blood in Scotland.' (caused war)
Buchan, *Witch Wood*

These examples show that, although the targets are understated, they still serve to emphasise the danger.

Fortunately, understatement is not restricted to violence and war. A powerful person may be said to have 'a little bit of influence' and when someone has given a generous donation to charity, they could be described as having made, 'a small contribution'. Scott understates Robin Hood's life of hunting and archery:

'He has twanged his bowstring right oft in merry Sherwood.'
Scott, *Ivanhoe*

EUPHEMISM
(YOU feh miz im)
Make harsh things more palatable

Euphemism is used when a more palatable way of addressing something unpleasant is required. It may describe someone as having a 'generous waistline' rather than being overweight or as being 'between jobs' rather than unemployed. When a film or book is described as 'of its time' it is most likely now perceived as racist or sexist.

Euphemisms are often employed politically; after all, it is much more polite for a powerful state to 'annex' rather than 'invade' another country and consequently to populate it with 'settlers' rather than 'colonists'. Soldiers would joke about a 'wooden discharge' being the only way to leave the army, meaning being sent home in a coffin. When slaughtered in battle they are described as 'the fallen' and may have been victims of 'friendly fire', whereas civilians killed by either side are 'collateral damage'. This kind of military spin is nothing new:

'The bones of his gallant army have whitened the sands of Palestine.'
Scott, *Ivanhoe*

Dying is the most popular subject for euphemism. The act is therefore referred to as 'passing away', 'being taken from us' or 'going to meet one's maker'. The state of being dead is spoken of as 'pushing up daisies', 'sleeping with the angels', 'no longer with us' or 'away to Davy Jones' Locker'. Dependent, of course, on particular social situations.

There are countless morbid euphemisms throughout literature:

'She wishes the baby and her too were in the churchyard.' (dead)
Hardy, *Tess of the d'Urbervilles*

'Abut ad plures.'
'He's gone to join the majority.' (dead)
Petronius, *Satyricon*

Death and killing are not the only targets of euphemism:

'I judge they are taking no chances of the jewelry evaporating.' (being stolen)
Runyon, *Little Pinks*

'The inhabitants appeared to have a propensity to throw any little trifles they were not in want of, into the road.' (household junk)
Dickens, *David Copperfield*

'A little smooth on the tooth in the matter of age.' (old)
Runyon, *Broadway Incident*

Euphemism may also employ metonymy to avoid mentioning unpleasant subjects. In the following example, Stevenson uses the dissection table to represent the corpses that have been stolen:

> 'The unclean and desperate interlopers who supplied the table.'
> Stevenson, *The Body-Snatcher*

DYSPHEMISM
(DIS Feh miz im)
Use of offensive or disparaging words

Whereas euphemism substitutes niceties to avoid unpleasant words, dysphemism does the opposite and presents us with harsh or pejorative alternatives. Curses, swearing and insults are the simplest of dysphemisms but these can be positive as well as negative. Which of these senses is being employed may depend very much on the situation or circumstances of usage and, of course, whether offence is intended.

Negative Dysphemism

In its most prevalent sense, dysphemism uses disparaging words to demean: 'cannon fodder' for soldiers, 'gutter press' for sensationalist newspapers, the 'butcher's apron' for the Union Flag and the 'slammer' for prison. Of course, many examples refer to death. Rather than opting for the the euphemism, 'pushing up daisies', a dead person would be dysphemistically described as 'food for the worms', 'belly up' or 'getting smoked'.

Many negative expressions are used to denigrate people. These insults vary widely from Dickens' physical description of an overweight boy in *The Pickwick Papers* as 'the bloated lad' to the political epithet for someone against Irish freedom in Joyce's *Dubliners*, 'I didn't think you were a West Briton.'

> 'Out, strumpet! Weep'st thou for him to my face?'
> (Desdemona)
> Shakespeare, *Othello*

> 'The tumultuous outcries and shouts of the rabble.'
> (people)
> Scott, *Old Mortality*

'I don't take kindly to the breed.' (lawyers)
Dickens, *Bleak House*

Some professions are targeted frequently with dysphemism. Psychiatrists are described as 'shrinks', journalists as 'hacks' and personal injury lawyers as 'ambulance chasers'. Doctors are targeted as 'quacks' amongst a variety of other names:

'No Christian leech within the four seas.'
Scott, *Ivanhoe*

'I saw that Sawbones turned sick and white with the desire to kill him.'
Stevenson, *Jekyll and Hyde*

Positive Dysphemism

Sometimes known as 'euphemistic dysphemism', this can be found in everyday speech such as addressing a close friend as an 'old rogue', describing ageing or being ill as having 'one foot in the grave' or perhaps praising someone's attire by saying, 'those shoes are wicked'. Getting married is frequently referred to as 'getting hitched' and a exciting party could later be described as having been a 'riot' or a 'blast'. It is also used with a kind of light-hearted bravado when cigarettes are nicknamed 'coffin nails' or 'cancers'.

Of course, depending on the circumstances and the company, most negative dysphemisms may be used lightheartedly when we are sure that no one will take offence. Such is the power of irony.

TAPINOSIS
(tah pi NO sis)
To belittle by understatement

Tapinosis is used to understate with intent to belittle or humiliate. For instance, one could describe David Bowie as 'Iggy Pop's piano player' or Buzz Aldrin as 'Neil Armstrong's driver' but, although these statements are essentially true, the great men are being denied their deserved merits. Dismissing the Taj Mahal as just a marble tombstone works in the same way. Tapinosis can be employed metaphorically to belittle another's grievance as 'a storm in a teacup' or their subsequent anger by saying, 'the rattle's out of the pram' or that they have 'spat the dummy'. It is used to dismiss environmental activists as 'tree-huggers' or people involved in charity work as 'do-gooders'. As far as occupational tapinoses go, a joiner can be referred to as a 'chippy', a mechanic as a 'grease monkey' and a prison officer as a 'turnkey'. All of these examples, although accurate, are somewhat demeaning.

LITOTES
(lie TOH tees)
Negation of the opposite for effect

Litotes is a figure of irony in which one thing is negated to affirm the opposite. When someone says that things are 'not bad' or that they 'wouldn't say no to a million dollars', they are using litotes. Many examples are found in everyday speech and in conjunction with other figures: 'it's not rocket science', 'I wouldn't say he was the sharpest knife in the drawer' or 'her contribution to the task was less than helpful'. When British Airways left hundreds of passengers stranded recently, it was remarked that 'it was not their finest hour'.

In *Maybe a Queen*, Runyon's narrator produces the litotic euphemism, 'Ida Peters is by no means a raving beauty', gently letting us know that she is rather ugly. Litotes can also produce positive understatement: in *Dubliners*, Joyce describes a character as 'not without culture' thus using double-negative litotes to inform us that the person is extremely cultured.

Litotes can employ a wide variety of negations such as 'not', 'no' and 'never'. However, litotes need not always be a complete negation; reductive phrases are also employed such as 'far from' or 'less than'. There are three main forms of litotes:

Oppositional Litotes	'Not', 'no', 'never', 'by no means'
Reductive Litotes	'Not exactly', 'far from' etc.
Double-Negative Litotes	'Not un-', 'not in-'

Oppositional Litotes

Litotes using 'Not'

'He was not the model boy of the village.'
   Twain, *Tom Sawyer*

'John Guidyill's temper was not improved by his decline in rank and increase in years.'
   Scott, *Old Mortality*

'The street was not as desirable a one as I could have wished it to be.'
   Dickens, *David Copperfield*

'And, to deal plainly, I fear I am not in my perfect mind.'
   Shakespeare, *King Lear*

'I love not these vanities.'
   Scott, *Ivanhoe*

'His line of life had not been the shortest distance between two points.'
   Joyce, *Dubliners*

'I cannot say the likeness was striking.'
   Dickens, *David Copperfield*

'The nobility hesitated not.'
   Scott, *Ivanhoe*

'To ride in such a carriage cannot be numbered among the things that appertain to glory.'
   Stevenson, *The Treasure of Franchard*

Litotes using 'No'

'Hesitation formed no part of Mr Alfred Jingle's character.'
   Dickens, *The Pickwick Papers*

'With no moderate hand.'
Scott, *Ivanhoe*

Litotes using 'By no means'

'She is likewise tender-hearted and benevolent, qualities for which her mistress is by no means remarkable.'
Smollett, *The Expedition of Humphry Clinker*

'She is by no means an old Judy and by no means bad looking.'
Runyon, *A Piece of Pie*

'The parrot lets go with a string of language that is by no means pure.'
Runyon, *So You Won't Talk*

'By no means of a slim figure.'
Dickens, *Oliver Twist*

'By no means incommoded with luggage.'
Dickens, *Bleak House*

Litotes using 'Never'

'I was never one of your bright ones.'
Joyce, *Ulysses*

Reductive Litotes

Litotes using 'Not exactly' and other adverbs:

'She was not exactly what the world calls young.'
Dickens, *Martin Chuzzlewit*

'Incidents in Rudolph's early career that may not be entirely to his credit.'
Runyon, *Johnny One-Eye*

'The hair-breadth twists and turns we made, drew down upon us a variety of speeches from the people standing about, which were not always complimentary.'
Dickens, *David Copperfield*

Litotes using 'Far From':

'[Mrs. Baynard] had actually fallen into the disease of buying pictures and antiques upon her own judgement, which was far from being infallible.'
 Smollett, *The Expedition of Humphry Clinker*

'Thaddeus T.'s former home life is far from being a plug for matrimony.'
 Runyon, *A Light in France*

'By this time, Rudolph is really far from being in the pink of condition.'
 Runyon, *Johnny One-Eye*

'Dancing, at which I must say I proved far from ornamental.'
 Stevenson, *Catriona*

'I can tell from Mrs News' conversation that she is far from being as intellectual as Professor Einstein.'
 Runyon, *Broadway Incident*

Double-Negative Litotes

This is a much less complex form of litotes in which 'not' and a prefixed word that uses 'un' or 'in' simply cancel each other out.

Litotes with Prefix:

'The auctioneer was not an ungenerous man.'
 Eliot, *Middlemarch*

'I have not treated her ungenerously.'
 Doyle, *The Noble Bachelor*

'His misfortunes, justly deserved as they were, were not unlamented.'
 Buchan, *Witch Wood*

'A contrast, not uncommon in matrimonial cases.'
 Dickens, *Oliver Twist*

'Mr Sherlock Holmes, who was usually very late in the mornings, save upon those not infrequent occasions when he stayed up all night, was seated at the breakfast table.'
    Doyle, *The Hound of the Baskervilles*

'Mr Quale asked Ada and me, not inaudibly, whether he was not a great creature.'
    Dickens, *Bleak House*

'I am not unaware, that, as Envy always dogs Merit at the heels there may be those who will whisper.'
    Scott, *Old Mortality*

'This was a not infrequent procedure with Mr Vincy.'
    Eliot, *Middlemarch*

'It is not unreasonable to conclude that something of an unreasonable nature has occurred meanwhile.'
    Dickens, *The Pickwick Papers*

'I am not unmindful that some of you have come here out of great trials and tribulations.'
    Martin Luther King

'I was far from being incurious or uninterested about the building.'
    Dickens, *Bleak House*

'An influence over her which may have been love or may have been fear, or very possibly both, since they are by no means incompatible emotions.'
    Doyle, *The Hound of the Baskervilles*

Litotes - Simile:
    There is also a particular form of litotes which produces a simile. When 'not' is combined with both 'un' and 'like' to produce 'not unlike', the double negative cancels itself out leaving a positive comparison: 'she was not unlike a poisonous snake' or 'it was not unlike being locked in a prison cell'. In the following example, Dickens could just as easily have used 'like':

> 'Mr Chadband moves softly and cumbrously, not unlike a bear who has been taught to walk upright.'
> Dickens, *Bleak House*

This litotes-simile effect also works with synonymous negatives:

> 'Our Aunt Tabitha, who had lost her cap in the struggle, and being more than half frantic, with rage and terror, was no bad representation of one of the sister Furies that guard the gates of hell.'
> Smollett, *The Expedition of Humphry Clinker*

Other Examples of Litotes:

> 'She therefore, watched his motions with feelings of intense terror, which were in no degree diminished by his coming close up to her.'
> Dickens, *The Pickwick Papers*

> 'It may be doubted whether his communication went a far way to increase Wilfrid's disposition to sympathise with the mourners of Coningsburgh.'
> Scott, *Ivanhoe*

> 'There is small friendship and scant courtesy between them and the boors of this country.'
> Scott, *Old Mortality*

> 'You can see by her voice, she is scarcely a singer by trade.'
> Runyon, *Neat Strip*

Multiple Litotes:

Occasionally, a writer will present more than one litotes in a sentence:

> 'It was not very skilfully done, but Winston's standards in such matters were not high.'
> Orwell, *Nineteen Eighty-Four*

'His choice has no less proved that his eyes are none of the clearest.'
    Scott, *Ivanhoe*

However, the prize goes, without any arguement, to Damon Runyon who presents us with three litotes in a single sentence:

'Maury is placed in this quicklime by certain parties who do not wish him well, and it is also the consensus of opinion that placing him there is by no means a bad idea, at that, as Maury is really quite a scamp and of no great credit to the community.'
    Runyon, *A Light in France*

Figures of Opposition
Paradox, Oxymoron, Antithesis, Antiphrasis

PARADOX
(PAH rah doks)
An absurd idea makes sense

Paradox is a figure in which a self-contradictory statement ironically rings true. At first glance, Cicero's great maxim, 'Silence is one of the great arts of conversation', can seem absurd but after a little thought the conflict is easily reconciled. Paradoxes such as 'conspicuous by their absence' and 'less is more' have now become idiomatic along with some classics:

'I must be cruel, only to be kind.'
Shakespeare, *Hamlet*

'We are condemned to be free.'
Jean Paul Sartre

'He has no enemies, but is intensely disliked by his friends.'
Oscar Wilde

'The chosen lie would pass into the permanent records and become truth.'
Orwell, *Nineteen Eighty-Four*

'I can resist everything except temptation.'
Wilde, *Lady Windermere's Fan*

'It is, of course, a trifle, but there is nothing so important as trifles.'
Doyle, *The Man with the Twisted Lip*

Life and death is a popular pairing for paradoxes:

'To sue to live, I find I seek to die;
And, seeking death, find life: let it come on.'
Shakespeare, *Measure for Measure*

'Now that he had recognised himself as a dead man it became important to stay alive as long as possible.'
Orwell, *Nineteen Eighty-Four*

Unlike oxymoron, paradox need not always include opposing words; it is the overall idea that brings about the irony by presenting conflict in a new light:

'All animals are equal, but some animals are more equal than others.'
Orwell, *Animal Farm*

'Another victory like that and we are done for.'
Joyce, *Ulysses*

'A business that makes nothing but money is a poor business.'
Henry Ford

'One must be poor to know the luxury of giving.'
Eliot, *Middlemarch*

'Water, water, everywhere, nor any drop to drink'
Coleridge, *The Rime of the Ancient Mariner*

OXYMORON
(ock see MOE ron)
Juxtaposition of contradictory ideas

Oxymoron is best described as condensed paradox. The difference being that the juxtaposition of the opposites in oxymoron produces the ironic clash with much more brevity. For example, in *Frankenstein*, Mary Shelley brings two opposing feelings together: 'That would be a cruel kindness'; the ironic combination of the contradictory terms works to develop a new understanding.

In everyday speech, oxymorons are often created intentionally to highlight contradictions: 'deafening silence', 'open secret', 'definitely maybe', 'working holiday, 'living dead, 'good grief'. At times, the clash of ideas may be accidental: 'live recording', 'new classic', 'critical acclaim', 'plastic glasses', 'mandatory option'.

Oxymorons combine a variety of parts of speech:

Adjective - Noun:

'Only served to make darkness visible.'
   Hogg, *The Brownie of Bodsbeck*

'A terrible beauty is born.'
   Yeats, *Easter 1916*

'Thou ev'n brightens dark Despair wi' gloomy smile.'
   Burns, *Scotch Drink*

'They have a plentiful lack of wit.'
   Shakespeare, *Hamlet*

'A tedious brief scene of young Pyramus
And his love Thisbe; very tragical mirth.'
   Shakespeare, *A Midsummer Night's Dream*

'It is a street of such dismal grandeur.'
   Dickens, *Bleak House*

'This picture brought such an agony of pleasurable suffering.'
   Twain, *Tom Sawyer*

'Her voice... charged with a sort of happy melancholy.'
   Orwell, *Nineteen Eighty-Four*

'She had a thrilling but delightful fear that Mr Seeders would rush in suddenly and shoot her with a pistol.'
   O Henry, *The Brief Debut of Tildy*

'I do here make humbly bold to present them with a short account of themselves and their art.'
   Swift, *Tale of a Tub*

'An odd kind of shabby luxury.'
   Dickens, *Bleak House*

'The whole countenance of nature... a face of awful joy.'
   Stevenson, *Olalla*

'The longer one stays here the more does the spirit of the moor sink into one's soul, its vastness, and also its grim charm.'
  Doyle, *The Hound of the Baskervilles*

'He was a long lean fellow… whose sullen face was redeemed by a humorous mouth, so that the impression was of a genial ferocity.'
  Buchan, *Witch Wood*

'That thou - O awful loveliness.'
  Shelley, *Hymn to Intellectual Beauty*

Gerund (Verb as Adjective) - Noun:

What art thou, Freedom? O, could slaves
Answer from their living graves.
  Shelley, *The Mask of Anarchy*

'Bring this waking nightmare to an end.'
  Stevenson, *Treasure of Franchard*

Adverb - Adjective:

'A wonderfully grave, precise and handsome piece of old china she looks.'
  Dickens, *Bleak House*

His honour rooted in dishonour stood,
And faith unfaithful kept him falsely true.
  Tennyson, *Lancelot and Elaine*

'That charmingly horrible person.'
  Dickens, *Bleak House*

'It was terribly beautiful to Tess today.'
  Hardy, *Tess of the d'Urbervilles*

Other combinations:

'Excessive sorrow laughs. Excessive joy weeps.'
  Blake, *The Marriage of Heaven and Hell*

'He bravely bore his miseries three weeks, and then one day turned up missing.'
    Twain, *Tom Sawyer*

'Thy wit is a very bitter sweeting; it is a most sharp sauce.'
    Shakespeare, *Romeo and Juliet*

Incongruous Oxymorons

Some combinations may simply be in disagreement rather than strict opposition:

'Dorothea had felt a delicious sad repose in their relation to each other.'
    Eliot, *Middlemarch*

'Good night, good night! parting is such sweet sorrow.'
    Shakespeare, *Romeo and Juliet*

'Bring him his gildit weapon.'
    Hogg, *Confessions of a Justified Sinner*

'He could swear wonderfully.'
    Twain, *Tom Sawyer*

'There will be a mournful glory shining in the place.'
    Dickens, *Bleak House*

Inexact-adjacency

On occasion the oxymoronic words are not positioned contiguously. Smaller parts of speech are sometimes used between them. However, the opposites should still have a combined effect. For example, the phrase, 'pleasure and pain' is not oxymoronic because the words are merely presented together. However, the same two words are combined in Walter Scott's *Marmion* to create an oxymoron: 'There is pleasure in this pain'.

'I passed three days in a luxury of wretchedness.'
    Dickens, *David Copperfield*

'With mirth in funeral and with dirge in marriage.'
    Shakespeare, *Hamlet*

'All in a perfect harmony of ugliness.'
Brown, *The House with the Green Shutters*

'Vagrant and triumphant life.'
Joyce, *Dubliners*

Accidental Oxymorons
There are also many ingenuous combinations which are subsequently interpreted cynically or politically as oxymorons: 'military intelligence', 'religious toleration', 'Microsoft Works, 'happily married', 'council worker', 'responsible gambling'. These couplings are only made incongruous by sarcastic interpretation. Although they should not be regarded as true oxymorons their entertainment value has to be appreciated.

ANTITHESIS
(an TIH thi sis)
Contrast of ideas in balanced phrases

Antithesis contrasts ideas in two balanced phrases, clauses or sentences. The equilibrium and rhythm of this figure work together to make a powerful literary tool. The balanced phrases also provide a sense of completeness that is extremely useful in constructing in proverbs such as 'to err is human, to forgive divine' and popular sayings like 'giving with one hand and taking away with the other'. Oscar Wilde would often use antithesis in his famous quips: 'The play was a great success but the audience was a total failure.' Martin Luther King employed antithesis with much more gravitas when he said: 'Live together as brothers or perish together as fools.' The paired ideas presented in antithesis may be polar opposites or simply contrasted by degree.

Antithesis of Opposition

'Willing to wound, and yet afraid to strike.'
Pope, *Epistle to Dr. Arbuthnot*

And neither the angels in Heaven above
Nor the demons down under the sea.
Poe, *Annabel Lee*

'Drown desperate sorrow in dead Edward's grave
And plant your joys in living Edward's throne.'
    Shakespeare, *Richard III*

'Cowards die many times before their deaths;
The valiant never taste death but once.'
    Shakespeare, *Julius Caesar*

Some truth there was, but dash'd and brew'd with lyes;
To please the fools and puzzle all the wise.
    Dryden, *Absalom and Achitophel*

'Marriage has many pains, but celibacy has no pleasures.'
    Johnson, *The History of Rasselas*

'Better to reign in Hell than serve in Heaven.'
    Milton, *Paradise Lost*

'Do not as some ungracious pastors do,
Show me the steep and thorny way to heaven,
Whiles, like a puff'd and reckless libertine,
Himself the primrose path of dalliance threads.'
    Shakespeare, *Hamlet*

Antithesis of Degree

'That's one small step for man, one giant leap for mankind.'
    Neil Armstrong

'Float like a butterfly, sting like a bee.'
    Muhammad Ali

'Not that I loved Caesar less, but that I loved Rome more.'
    Shakespeare, *Julius Caesar*

(The balanced structure of antithesis means that many cases are also examples of bicolon.)

ANTIPHRASIS
(an TIF ra sis)
Ironic substitution of an opposite

Antiphrasis is the term for a word or phrase being used to mean the exact opposite. It is the backbone sarcasm in phrases such as: 'take your time' when someone is going too slowly, 'thanks a bunch', after some disservice or, 'that was really clever', when they have done something stupid.

Unlike euphemism, there is no attempt to make what is being said more palatable. The opposite words used, serve to criticise the person or situation ironically and are usually positive substitutions for negative intentions:

'He seems a very amiable person.' (after Holmes is
threatened by large adversary)
    Doyle, *The Speckled Band*

'His affectionate friend.' (Sikes after he threatens Fagin.)
    Dickens, *Oliver Twist*

'The noble Brutus
Hath told you Caesar was ambitious:
If it were so, it was a grievous fault,
And grievously hath Caesar answer'd it.
Here, under leave of Brutus and the rest
For Brutus is an honourable man.'
    Shakespeare, *Julius Caesar*

'A nice paper to put into a girl's hand.'(fake marriage certificate)
    Stevenson, *The Beach of Falesá*

'Sirrah, you giant, what says the doctor to my water?' (Falstaff to his young page)
    Shakespeare, *Henry IV*

Figures of Ambiguity
Paronomasia, Antanaclasis, Adianoeta

PARONOMASIA (PUN)
(par oh noh MEY zhah)
Play on similar sounding words

Of all the ironies, this device can produce not only the most humorous results but also the most cringeworthy. Paronomasia, more commonly known as 'pun', employs the ambiguity of sounds of words and phrases. For example, in *Romeo and Juliet*, the hero declares: 'You have dancing shoes with nimble soles; I have a soul of lead, / So stakes me to the ground I cannot move'. Here Shakespeare uses two different words with the same pronunciation yet brings them together in a single idea. This kind of play on words can be found throughout literature, songwriting, comedy and film.

> "You see the earth takes twenty-four hours to turn round on its axis."
> "Talking of axes," said the Duchess, "chop off her head!"
> Carroll, *Alice's Adventures in Wonderland*

Paronomasias may also be used to emphasise irony in more dramatic situations. It was one of the many figures mastered by Shakespeare and he was not shy of employing pun even in the darkest of scenes such as when Lady Macbeth plans to smear the servants faces with blood: 'I'll gild the faces of the grooms withal, For it must seem their guilt.'

> 'Now is the winter of our discontent,
> Made glorious summer by this Son of York.'
> Shakespeare, *Richard III*

> 'Driving out of the Mansion House… in all my vermin.'
> (ermine)
> Joyce, *Dubliners*

ANTANACLASIS
(an tan a KLAS is)
Repeated use of homonyms

Antanaclasis is the ironic use of homonyms. Whereas in paronomasia the sounds of words and word clusters are alike but not necessarily the same, in antanaclasis the words are identical but used in different senses. The difference between the two figures can be exemplified in this Shakespearian quote:

> 'Yea, and so used it that were it not here apparent that
> thou art heir apparent.'
> Shakespeare, *Henry IV*

This exchange between Falstaff and Prince Hal is antanaclasic by the use of 'apparent' in two different senses. However, it also employs paronomasia by the rather tenuous phonetic similarity of 'here' and 'heir'. Despite the more precise definition, antanaclasis is often categorised as a type of pun. However, it can always be recognised as a discrete figure by the repeated homonyms:

> 'Your argument is sound, nothing but sound.'
> Benjamin Franklin

> 'In thy youth learn some craft that in thy age thou mayest
> get thy living without craft.'
> Samuel Johnson

> 'To England I'll steal and there I'll steal.'
> Shakespeare, *Henry V*

ADIANOETA
(ah dee ah NOH tah)
Expressing a subtle double meaning

Of all the ironies, adianoeta is the one that truly requires context. Someone having watched a particularly bad show may afterwards say to the actor involved: 'Your performance was outstanding'; this will most likely be taken as a compliment, but it could also be a hidden criticism; perhaps the actor was outstandingly bad. This is the root of adianoeta: it is an expression that says one thing but also has a secondary meaning lurking in the background. It differs from the sarcasm of antiphrasis by its ingenuous delivery. For example, when a rather useless colleague announces they are moving on, someone may say, 'I am sad to hear you'll be leaving next month' when they really mean, 'I wish you had left a long time ago'. Another example would be to remark to a writer friend, 'I look forward to having your new book on my shelf.'

Towards the end of one Sherlock Holmes story there is an exchange between a pretentious monarch and the detective when they discover they have been outwitted by a rather smart lady:

> "Is it not a pity she was not on my level?"
> "From what I have seen of the lady, she seems, indeed, to be on a very different level to your majesty."
> Doyle, *A Scandal in Bohemia*

At times, adianoetas may be thinly veiled, as when someone says, 'I hope you have the Christmas you deserve'. On the other hand they may be extremely subtle. To end each of his shows, the Irish comedian, Dave Allen, who famously described himself as a practicing atheist, would use the same religious sounding line: 'And may your God go with you'; which may have been adianoeta or just a polite goodbye. One of the most famous opening lines in literature is an adianoeta:

> 'It is a truth universally acknowledged, that a single man in possession of a good fortune, must be in want of a wife.'
> Austen, *Pride and Prejudice*

> 'I used your soap two years ago; since then I have used no other.'
> Tramp in vintage Pears' Soap advertisement

> 'And for cookin' there's no' his equal.'
> Munro, *Para Handy*

When the double meaning becomes too obvious, we are entering the world of innuendo.

The Metaphoric Manual

Schemes

Unlike tropes, schemes do not actually change meaning; they simply foreground ideas by means of unusual arrangement. Whilst many writers avoid unnecessary repetition, it can sometimes be useful to focus attention on certain words or phrases. Schemes may also present words in an unorthodox fashion; verbs can be shared with incongruous nouns and words can be presented ungrammatically, split or omitted to disrupt the flow of the text.

Schemes are presented in four categories: Repetition; parallelism; disruption; omission and sharing.

Figures of Repetition

Epizeuxis, Diacope, Epanalepsis, Anadiplosis, Polyptoton, Chiasmus, Antimetabole, Anaphora, Epiphora, Symploce, Mesodiplosis

EPIZEUXIS
(eh pi ZOOK sis)
Immediate repetition of a word

Epizeuxis is a scheme in which a word or short phrase is repeated immediately. It is a simple yet effective way of focusing on a particular idea and can be used as an emotive building block, to enhance exclamations, to elongate an experience or simply to fade away. However, like all schemes of repetition, it should be used with care; it is not simply a matter of repeating words randomly. For instance, when Robert Burns chose to describe a 'red, red rose,' he was not struggling to find alternative adjectives, but emphasising the simplicity and singularity of the rose. In the first of the following examples, Dickens uses epizeuxis in the same way to dwell on an adjective:

'Pleasant, pleasant country.'
　　Dickens, *The Pickwick Papers*

'It launch'd forth filament, filament, filament, out of itself.'
　　Whitman, *A Noiseless Patient Spider*

'No, no - there are depths, depths!'
　　James, *The Turn of the Screw*

Alone, alone, all, all alone,
Alone on a wide wide sea!
　　Coleridge, *The Rime of the Ancient Mariner*

'What! A commoner send a challenge to a peer of the realm? Privilege! Privilege!'
　　Smollett, *The Expedition of Humphry Clinker*

'But why, why, why?'
   Shakespeare, *Anthony and Cleopatra*

'Touch me. Soft eyes. Soft soft soft hand. I am lonely here.'
   Joyce, *Ulysses*

'Then I went on, thinking, thinking, thinking; and the fire went on, burning, burning, burning.'
   Dickens, *Bleak House*

'You must be Independent, Independent, Independent… go your own way and let your neighbour go his.'
   Charles Rennie Mackintosh

Short phrases can be used and conjunctions may sometimes link the repeated words:

'The horror! The horror!'
   Conrad, *Heart of Darkness*

'Tomorrow, and tomorrow, and tomorrow.'
   Shakespeare, *Macbeth*

'Never' has always been a popular choice for immediate repetition. Never-Never Land is an imaginary place where everything is perfect, but it is also used for the 'Never Never' which is slang for debt that may never be paid off.

'Bold Lover, never, never canst thou kiss.'
   Keats, *Ode on a Grecian Urn*

'Nobody will see him again, never, never, never.'
   Conrad, *Heart of Darkness*

'Thou'lt come no more
Never, never, never, never, never!'
   Shakespeare, *King Lear*

DIACOPE
(die AH koh peh)
Repetition with intervening words

Diacope is a scheme in which a word or phrase is repeated after intervening words. For example, 'the shame. The utter shame of it!' Whereas epizeuxis works through immediate repetition, diacope allows a short breathing space before returning to the idea. Diacope serves a variety of functions: it can be employed emotively to refocus on words, use repetition for comic effect or to establish a linking structure for surrounding ideas:

'I see the necessity of departure; and it is like looking on the necessity of death.'
Brontë, *Jane Eyre*

The target words may be placed anywhere within the sentence or in a nearby sentence, although when they occur only at the beginning and end the correct term is epanalepsis. Diacope works with most parts of speech and with longer phrases:

Diacope of Nouns:

'In this place you could not feel anything, except pain and the foreknowledge of pain.'
Orwell, *Nineteen Eighty-Four*

'There is a superstition in avoiding superstition.'
Francis Bacon

'The answer to injustice is not to silence the critic but to end the injustice.'
Paul Robeson

'Five years have past; five summers, with the length of five long winters!'
Wordsworth, *Tintern Abbey*

Diacope of Adjectives:

'To run this desperate course with desperate men.'
Scott, *Old Mortality*

'I suppose I am a bad fellow - a damn bad fellow. I was born bad, and I have lived bad, and I shall die bad in all probability.'
    Hardy, *Tess of the d'Urbervilles*

'I'll be as dirty as I please, and I like to be dirty, and I will be dirty!'
    Brontë, *Wuthering Heights*

Diacope of Verbs:

O wad some pow'r the giftie gie us
To see oursels as others see us
    Burns, *To a Louse*

'Tis better to have loved and lost
Than never to have loved at all.
    Tennyson, *In Memoriam AHH*

'Tread softly because you tread on my dreams.'
    Yeats, *Aedh Wishes for the Cloths of Heaven*

'The Party is not concerned with perpetuating its blood but with perpetuating itself.'
    Orwell, *Nineteen Eighty-Four*

Diacope with mixed Parts of Speech:

'Gathering her brows like gathering storm.'
    Burns, *Tam O'Shanter*

'I pray thee, chide not; she whom I love now
Doth grace for grace and love for love allow.'
    Shakespeare, *Romeo and Juliet*

Diacope of Phrases:

'But of course I do not ask any questions, as the best you can get from asking questions along Broadway is a reputation for asking questions.'
    Runyon, *So You Won't Talk*

'A ruling group is a ruling group so long as it can nominate its successors.'
   Orwell, *Nineteen Eighty-Four*

'He livens up quite some and begins taking an interest in his surroundings and talking about the good old days, but as near as I can make out, Blooch's good old days are about the same as everybody else's good old days and most of the time he is half starving.'
   Runyon, *Big Shoulders*

'The Clerkinwell Sessions have brought it upon themselves, ma'am... and if the Clerkinwell Sessions find that they come off rather worse than they expected, the Clerkinwell Sessions have only themselves to thank.'
   Dickens, *Oliver Twist*

'I've seen the devil of violence, and the devil of greed, and the devil of hot desire.'
   Conrad, *Heart of Darkness*

(If the repeated word is a homonym and is used ironically in a different sense - the fugure is antanaclasis.)

EPANALEPSIS
(eh pah nah LEP sis)
Beginning and ending with the same words.

Epanalepsis is a scheme in which a sentence or passage begins and ends in the same way. It can create a powerful statement enclosed in a parenthesis of words. Structurally, it is found in single sentences, consecutive sentences, paragraphs or stanzas, and may employ single words or phrases:

One word Epanalepsis:

'Blow, winds, and crack your cheeks! rage! blow!'
   Shakespeare, *King Lear*

'Delicacy, my dear friend. Delicacy.'
   Dickens, *The Pickwick Papers*

'Inferiority! I never had such a sentiment as a feeling of inferiority!'
Hogg, *The Three Perils of Man*

'Airs romped around him, nipping and eager airs.'
Joyce, *Ulysses*

'Want?...What does it matter what you want?'
Brown, *The House with the Green Shutters*

'Blood hath bought blood, and blows have answer'd blows.'
Shakespeare, *King John*

Phrasal Epanalepsis:

'To be or not to be?'
Shakespeare, *Hamlet*

'Weep no more, woeful shepherds, weep no more.'
Milton, *Lycidas*

'Once more unto the breach, dear friends, once more.'
Shakespeare, *Henry V*

'To be hanged by the neck, till he was dead - that was the end. To be hanged by the neck until he was dead.'
Dickens, *Oliver Twist*

ANADIPLOSIS
(an ah di PLOH sis)
Ending of one clause is the beginning of the next

When a word or phrase is used to end a sentence or clause and the same word is immediately repeated to begin the next, the term is anadiplosis. Anadiplosis thus creates a sense of continuance or linkage between larger ideas:

'For Lycidas is dead, dead ere his prime.'
Milton, *Lycidas*

> 'Rocks turn to rivers, rivers turn to men.'
> Herrick, *To Dean Bourn*

> I kissed the rod, / Hand rather, my heart lo! lapped strength, stole joy, would laugh, chéer. / Cheer whom though?
> Hopkins, *Carrion Comfort*

> Under the light, yet under
> Under the grass and the dirt…
> Over the light, yet over,
> Over the arc of the bird. (also epanalepsis)
> Dickinson, *Under the Light, Yet Under*

> 'This late age of world's experience had bred in them all, all men and women, a well of tears. Tears and sorrows.'
> Woolf, *Mrs Dalloway*

Anadiplosis often includes longer phrases:

> 'Every branch of study or subject of conversation skirted forbidden ground. Forbidden ground was the question of the return of the dead.'
> James, *The Turn of the Screw*

> 'Here she is mending her dress; mending her dress as usual.'
> Woolf, *Mrs Dalloway*

Anadiplosis can also link verses and stanzas:

> So fair are thou my bonnie lass,
> So deep in love am I
> And I will love thee still, my dear,
> Till a' the seas gang dry.
>
> Till a' the seas gang dry, my dear,
> And rocks melt wi' the sun,
> And I will love thee still, my dear
> While the sands of life shall run.
> Burns, *Red, Red Rose*

Here, Burns uses the figure not only for continuance but for augmentation; the ending of one verse is a platform for the next. Anadiplosis can be used in this way to build a series of phrases:

> 'A whore can govern the backstairs, the backstairs a council, and the council a senate.'
> Swift, *Gulliver's Travels*

> 'A pot. A pot is a beginning of a rare bit of trees. Trees tremble, the old vats are in bobbles, bobbles which shade and shove and render clean, render clean must.'
> Stein, *Susie Asado*

POLYPTOTON
(poh LIP toh ton)
Repetition of a word in a different part of speech or tense

Rather than exact repetition, polyptoton repeats a word but in a different part of speech or tense. For example, a popular axiom attributed to Socrates informs us that 'the unexamined life is not worth living'; the words, 'life' and 'living' have the same root. Lord Acton uses a double polyptoton in his insightful political quote: 'Power tends to corrupt, and absolute power corrupts absolutely.'

The parts of speech, cases or conjugations used in polyptota are numerous:

> 'I have not broken your heart - you have broken it; and in breaking it, you have broken mine.'
> Brontë, *Wuthering Heights*

> 'She is only talking to hear herself talk.'
> Runyon, *Maybe a Queen*

> 'They would all in a few years be as if they had never been.'
> Hardy, *Tess of the d'Urbervilles*

> 'It takes quite a little to displease my old man, but when he is displeased he is certainly greatly displeased.'
> Runyon, *Too Much Pep*

'Those who restrain desire do so because theirs is weak enough to be restrained.'
    Blake, *The Marriage of Heaven and Hell*

Have I forgot, my only love, to love thee,
Severed at last by Time's all-severing wave?
    Brontë, *Remembrance*

'It gleams betrayed and to betray.'
    Shelley, *Euganean Hills*

'I can understand his reluctance about pushing himself off. Personally, I will not care to push myself off. However… I hear it is against the law in Florida to push people off, even if they wish to be pushed.'
    Runyon, *A Job for the Macarone*

'Orthodoxy means not thinking - not needing to think.'
    Orwell, *Nineteen Eighty-Four*

'And I pray one prayer.'
    Brontë, *Wuthering Heights*

'So as not to offend the police commissioner in case he comes around looking for offense.'
    Runyon, *Neat Strip*

'Let the skaith fall upon the skaither.'
    Hogg, *The Three Perils of Man*

Princes, the dregs of their dull race, who flow
Through public scorn, mud from a muddy spring
    Shelley, *England in 1819*

'Hazel eyes which had that look of apprehension in them which makes complete strangers apprehensive too.'
    Woolf, *Mrs Dalloway*'

'The Greeks are strong, and skilful to their strength,
Fierce to their skill, and to their fierceness valiant.'
    Shakespeare, *Troilus and Cressida*

'She might be firm, and must be; but only in bearing their firmness, and firmly believing there was no other firmness upon earth.'
Dickens, *David Copperfield*

'Mr Jinks, who was busily engaged in looking as busy as possible.'
Dickens, *The Pickwick Papers*

'The sharp old lady, sharply shaking her head.'
Dickens, *Bleak House*

'I do not say that all of the wicked people in the world are along east 114th Street... , but the wicked people on east 114th Street are wickeder than somewhat.'
Runyon, *Too Much Pep*

Careless she is with artful care,
Affecting to seem unaffected.
Congreve, *Amoret*

CHIASMUS
(keh AS mus)
Structural symmetry

The name chiasmus is derived from the Greek word for the letter 'x'. This device inverts the word order of one phrase to produce a cross-over or reversal of the idea in the subsequent phrase. (It is also known as 'inverted parallelism' and 'syntactical inversion') The reflected ideas can be synonymous or contrasting. Taking an example from Shakespeare's *Othello*:

'Who dotes, yet doubts - suspects, yet soundly loves.'

Who dotes,	yet doubts -	suspects,	yet soundly loves.
A	B	B2	A2

When each part of this sentence is labelled, it can be seen that A2 reflects A - love/ dotes, and B2 reflects B - suspects/ doubts. The ideas in the line from Shakespeare are in agreement, whereas in the following example from Walter Scott, the ideas contrast:

'Let me die in peace if thou be mortal; if thou be a demon, thy time is not yet come.'
    Scott, *Ivanhoe*

'A man is but the product of his thoughts. What he thinks, he becomes.'
    Mahatma Gandhi

'Smooth flow the waves, the zephyrs gently play.'
    Pope, *The Rape of the Lock*

'Love without end, and without measure Grace.'
    Milton, *Paradise Lost*

'By day the frolic, and the dance by night.'
    Johnson, *The Vanity of Human Wishes*

Polish'd in Courts and harden'd in the Field,
Renown'd for Conquest, and in Council skill'd.
    Addison, *The Campaign*

ANTIMETABOLE
(an ti meh TAH bo leh)
Repetition of words in reverse order

Antimetabole is a type of chiasmus that follows the same pattern but reflects the exact words rather than the idea. Many recognisable phrases use this technique: 'when the going gets tough, the tough get going', 'if you fail to plan, then you plan to fail', 'once upon a time, the internet was an escape from the real world, now the real world is an escape from the internet'. Even *The Three Musketeers* used it for their motto: 'All for one, and one for all.'

'Fair is foul and foul is fair.'
    Shakespeare, *Macbeth*

'For the strength of the Pack is the Wolf, and the strength of the Wolf is the Pack.'
    Kipling, *The Jungle Book*

'Mankind must put an end to war, or war will put an end to mankind.'
    J. F. Kennedy

'Integrity without knowledge is weak and useless, and knowledge without integrity is dangerous and dreadful.'
    Johnson, *The History of Rasselas*

'It was not the thorn bending to the honeysuckles, but the honeysuckles embracing the thorn.'
    Brontë, *Wuthering Heights*

Words may be used in a different part of speech or slightly paraphrased for the reflection:

''Tis strange, but true; for truth is always strange.'
    Byron, *Don Juan*

'If you stare into the abyss, the abyss stares back at you.'
    Friedrich Nietzsche

'If black men have no rights in the eyes of the white men, of course, the whites can have none in the eyes of the blacks.'
    Frederick Douglass

'It is not the oath that makes us believe the man, but the man that makes us believe the oath.'
    Aeschylus

In the following examples from George Orwell, short phrases are reflected:

'One does not establish a dictatorship in order to safeguard a revolution; one makes the revolution in order to establish the dictatorship.'
    Orwell, *Nineteen Eighty-Four*

'Until they become conscious they will never rebel, and until after they rebel they cannot become conscious.'
    Orwell, *Nineteen Eighty-Four*

In the final example, Samuel Johnson, uses the reversal as a cutting critisism:

'Your manuscript is both good and original, but the part that is good is not original, and the part that is original is not good.'
Samuel Johnson

ANAPHORA
(ah NAH for ah)
Beginnings of consecutive sentences repeated

Anaphora is a figure of speech in which the opening words are repeated in successive clauses or sentences. For example:

'Blood built it; blood stopped the building of it; blood shall bring it down.'
Stevenson, *Kidnapped*

Here, Stevenson uses anaphora to build towards the portent of doom. This is also a popular structural technique in poetry and songwriting. Anaphora may use single words or longer phrases:

One Word Anaphora

Theirs not to make reply,
Theirs not to reason why,
Theirs but to do and die.
Tennyson, *The Charge of the Light Brigade*

Whiles holding fast his gude blue bonnet;
Whiles crooning o'er some auld Scots sonnet;
Whiles glowring round wi' prudent cares,
Lest bogles catch him unawares.
Burns, *Tam O'Shanter*

'My gold, my fortune, my felicity.'
Marlowe, *The Jew of Malta*

'No crime, no mischief, no malignity, no misery, can be found comparable to mine.'
Shelley, *Frankenstein*

'Welcome poverty… welcome misery, welcome houselessness, welcome hunger, rags, tempest and beggary!'
    Dickens, *David Copperfield*

'The forerunner of change, of conquest, of trade, of massacres, of blessings.'
    Conrad, *Heart of Darkness*

Phrasal Anaphora

My heart is like a singing bird
    Whose nest is in a water'd shoot;
My heart is like an apple-tree
    Whose boughs are bent with thick-set fruit;
My heart is like a rainbow shell
    That paddles in a halcyon sea;
My heart is gladder than all these,
    Because my love is come to me.
    Rossetti, *A Birthday*

In every cry of every man,
In every infant's cry of fear,
In every every voice, in every ban
The mind-forged manacles I hear.
    Blake, *London*

'A thought stung to my heart, a thought wounded me like a sword, a thought, like a worm in a flower, profaned the holiness of my love.'
    Stevenson, *Olalla*

'Twas Christmas broached the mightiest ale;
'Twas Christmas told the merriest tale.
    Scott, *Marmion*

'Rarely did that hour of the evening come, rarely did I wake at night, rarely did I look up at the moon or stars, or watch some falling rain, or hear the wind, but I thought of his solitary figure.'
    Dickens, *David Copperfield*

> Sweet was that error - sweeter still than death
> Sweet was that error - even with us the breath
> > Poe, *Al-Aaraaf*

> 'The more successful the villain, the more successful the picture.'
> > Alfred Hitchcock

> 'The more I see of the moneyed classes, the more I understand the guillotine.'
> > George Bernard Shaw

> 'There will be no loyalty, except loyalty to the Party. There will be no love, except the love of Big Brother. There will be no laughter, except the laugh of triumph over a defeated enemy. There will be no art, no literature, no science.'
> > Orwell, *Nineteen Eighty-Four*

> 'In spite of your own better reason - in spite of your friends' entreaties - in spite of the almost inevitable ruin which yawns before you.'
> > Scott, *Old Mortality*

> 'He was not like youth, he was not like age, he was not like anything in the world but a model of deportment.'
> > Dickens, *Bleak House*

One form of anaphora establishes a target in the middle of the first clause before repeating it at beginnings of subsequent clauses:

> 'Here was the same beautiful scene, the same abundant foliage, the same splendid palaces and magnificent ruins, the same river running between its fertile banks.'
> > Wells, *The Time Machine*

> 'One being who would be content to devote his whole existence to your happiness - who lives but in your eyes - who breathes but in your smiles - who bears the heavy burden of life itself only for you.'
> > Dickens, *The Pickwick Papers*

'Uriah looked at me, and looked at Agnes, and looked at the dishes, and looked at the plates, and looked at every object in the room.'
  Dickens, *David Copperfield*

EPIPHORA
(eh PIF oh ra)
Repeated endings in consecutive sentences

Whereas anaphora repeats beginnings of clauses or sentences, epiphora (also known as epistrophe) repeats the endings:

'I'll have my bond; speak not against my bond: I have sworn an oath that I will have my bond.'
  Shakespeare, *The Merchant of Venice*

'A fine woman! a fair woman! a sweet woman!'
  Shakespeare, *Othello*

'Mrs Parsons would be vaporized. Syme would be vaporized. Winston would be vaporized. O'Brien would be vaporized.'
  Orwell, *Nineteen Eighty-Four*

'But yet the pity of it, Iago! O Iago, the pity of it, Iago!'
  Shakespeare, *Othello*

An anthem for the queenliest dead
    that ever died so young
A dirge for her the doubly dead
    in that she died so young.
        Poe, *Lenore*

As of someone gently rapping,
    rapping at my chamber door.
''Tis some visitor,' I muttered,
    'tapping at my chamber door.'
        Poe, *The Raven*

In *The Raven*, Poe repeats endings in several couplets throughout but also uses epiphora to link most verses with

'Nevermore'. The same technique can be seen in Tennyson's *The Charge of the Light Brigade* where every stanza ends with, 'six hundred':

> …Into the valley of Death / Rode the six hundred.
> …Into the valley of Death / Rode the six hundred.
> …Into the mouth of hell / Rode the six hundred.
> …Then they rode back, but not / Not the six hundred.
> …All that was left of them, / Left of six hundred.
> …Honour the Light Brigade, / Noble six hundred!
> Tennyson, *The Charge of the Light Brigade*

(Epiphora and epistrophe are alternative words for the same device. However, it is much easier for students to remember the term epiphora because of its similarity to the opposite, anaphora.)

SYMPLOCE
(sim PLOES)
Repetition of anaphora and epiphora

Symploce is a combination of anaphora and epiphora: both the beginnings and endings of word groups are repeated. It is useful form to present or develop a series of linked ideas in a parenthetical framework. Nonetheless, the structure is quite flexible and the ideas enclosed may be anything from single words to entire sentences:

> Cannon to right of them,
> Cannon to left of them,
> Cannon in front of them.
> Tennyson, *Charge of the Light Brigade*

> 'Against yourself you are calling him,
> against the laws you are calling him,
> against the democratic constitution you are calling him.'
> Aeschines

> 'The madman is not the man who has lost his reason. The madman is the man who has lost everything except his reason.'
> Chesterton, *Orthodoxy*

'Whom the senate hath condemned, whom the people of
Rome have condemned, whom all men have condemned.'
    Cicero

The life upon her yellow hair, but not within her eyes
The life still there, upon her hair, the death upon her eyes.
    Poe, *Lenore*

'I went away, dear Agnes, loving you. I stayed away,
loving you. I returned home, loving you!'
    Dickens, *David Copperfield*

'Who is here so base that would be a bondman?
If any, speak; for him have I offended.
Who is here so rude that would not be a Roman?
If any, speak; for him have I offended.
Who is here so vile that will not love his country?
If any, speak; for him have I offended.'
    Shakespeare, *Julius Caesar*

One popular symploce, which has been adapted throughout the centuries, presents a chain of causation:

For want of a nail the shoe was lost.
For want of a shoe the horse was lost.
For want of a horse the rider was lost.
For want of a rider the battle was lost.
For want of a battle the kingdom was lost.
And all for the want of a horseshoe nail.
    Proverb

In the following example, Shakespeare adapts the scheme to enclose several further accusations within the third repetition:

'That Angelo's forsworn; is it not strange?
That Angelo's a murderer; is't not strange?
That Angelo is an adulterous thief,
An hypocrite, a virgin-violator;
Is it not strange and strange?'
    Shakespeare, *Measure for Measure*

An even longer symploce comes from Bartholomew Griffin:

Most true that I must fair Fidessa love.
Most true that I fair Fidessa cannot love.
Most true that I do feel the pains of love.
Most true that I am captive unto love.
Most true that I deluded am with love.
Most true that I do find the sleights of love.
Most true that nothing can procure her love.
Most true that I must perish in my love.
Most true that she contemns the god of love.
Most true that he is snared with her love.
Most true that she would have me cease to love.
Most true that she herself alone is love.
Most true that though she hated, I would love!
Most true that dearest life shall end with love.
    Griffin, *Fidessa, More Chaste Than Kinde*

MESODIPLOSIS
(mes oh dih PLOH sis)
Middles of sentences repeated

Mesodiplosis is the repetition of words or phrases in the middles of successive sentences. It is a close relation to anaphora and epiphora, and a structural opposite to symploce. Because of the focus of repetition on the middle of the sentence and the balance of words around, mesodiplosis can often result in examples of parallelism. The scheme is most effective when repeating small phrases or word groups, but a single word is often enough.

Single-Word Mesodiplosis

'In front of a big book-case, in a big chair, behind a big table, and before a big volume, sat Mr Nupkins, looking a full size larger than any one of them, big as they were.'
    Dickens, *The Pickwick Papers*

'The ripple of the river, the soughing of the trees swayed by the wind, the murmurs of the crowds.'
    Conrad, *Heart of Darkness*

'Oliver was frightened at the sight of so many gentlemen, which made him tremble; and the beadle gave him

another tap from behind, which made him cry; and these two causes made him answer in a very low and hesitating voice.'
    Dickens, *Oliver Twist*

Phrasal Mesodiplosis

'Fed with the same food, hurt with the same weapons, subject to the same diseases, healed by the same means, warmed and cooled by the same winter and summer.'
    Shakespeare, *The Merchant of Venice*

'Capable to kindle as well as melt, to command as well as to beseech.'
    Scott, *Ivanhoe*

'Pity is the feeling which arrests the mind in the presence of whatsoever is grave and constant in human sufferings and unites it with the sufferer. Terror is the feeling which arrests the mind in the presence of whatsoever is grave and constant in human sufferings and unites it with the secret cause.'
    Joyce, *A Portrait of the Artist as a Young Man*

Figures of Parallelism

Isocolon, Bicolon, Tricolon, Polysyndeton, Asyndeton, Parataxis, Hypotaxis

ISOCOLON
(AYE soh coh lon)
Balanced structure in successive phrases

Isocolon, also referred to as parallelism, indicates a repetition of syntax rather than individual words. For example:

'Think in the morning. Act in the noon. Eat in the evening. Sleep in the night.' (also mesodiplosis)
William Blake, *The Marriage of Heaven and Hell*

In these short sentences, although the prepositions and articles match, the main words are different. However, what ties the four sentences together is the similarity of structure. Although, in some cases, particular words are also repeated, it is primarily the arrangement of consecutive clauses or sentences that creates the desired effect.

Isocolon refers to any number of repeated structures but also includes two minor forms: bicolon - denoting a pair, and tricolon - a triplet of consecutive matching word units. These devices are used widely throughout literature, politics and everyday speech to create balance, climax, contrast or opposition. Although isocolonic statements often stand alone, they can also be part of longer sentences.

'He was pinched in, and swelled out, and got up, and strapped down, as much as he could possibly bear.'
Dickens, *Bleak House*

Isocolon includes not only bicolon and tricolon but also any number of structurally repeated word units:

'I'll give my jewels for a set of beads,
My gorgeous palace for a hermitage,
My gay apparel for an almsman's gown,
My figured goblets for a dish of wood,

My sceptre for a palmer's walking staff,
My subjects for a pair of carved saints
And my large kingdom for a little grave.'
    Shakespeare, *Richard II*

'My life has been a life of trouble and turmoil; of change and vicissitude; of anger and exultation; of sorrow and of vengeance.'
    Hogg, *Confessions of a Justified Sinner*

'On many such loungers have the speckled shadows of those trees often fallen; on the bent like head, the bitten nail, the lowering eye, the lingering step, the purposeless and dreamy air, the good consuming and consumed, the life turned sour.'
    Dickens, *Bleak House*

One of the most famous isocolons in literature can also be described as a series of antitheses:

'It was the best of times, it was the worst of times, it was the age of wisdom, it was the age of foolishness, it was the epoch of belief, it was the epoch of incredulity, it was the season of Light, it was the season of Darkness, it was the spring of hope, it was the winter of despair, we had everything before us, we had nothing before us, we were all going direct to Heaven, we were all going direct the other way.'
    Dickens, *A Tale of Two Cities*

Synathroesmus

Synathroesmus is a scheme closely related to isocolon in which different words are listed consecutively using the same part of speech. The words used are usually adjectives or verbs:

'He plunges at me, guttering, choking, drowning.'
    Owen, *Dulce et Decorum Est.*

'An old, mad, blind, despised and dying King.'
    Shelley, *England in 1819*

'Stout, simple, plain, clean, wholesome woman.'
  James, *The Turn of the Screw*

'This live, throbbing age,
That brawls, cheats, maddens, calculates, aspires.'
  Browning, *Aurora Leigh*

Many cases of isocolon, because they often repeat words at beginnings, middles and ends of sentences or clauses, are also examples of other schemes. (anaphora, epiphora, mesodiplosis, antimetabole, hypozeuxis)

BICOLON
(BI coh lon)
Balanced structure in two successive phrases

Bicolon is a form of isocolon in which two structurally similar sentences or clauses are positioned together. These may be found in short popular sayings such as 'least said, soonest mended', 'roses are red, violets are blue' or in Orwell's *Animal Farm* where they chant, 'Four legs good, two legs bad!'

Bicolon has two main uses: augmentation which uses the first clause as a platform for the second, and contrast, in which the two parts are discordant or opposite and often also examples of antithesis.

Augmented Bicolon

'By force to ravish, or by fraud betray.'
  Pope, *The Rape of the Lock*

By all the hate which checks a father's love
By all the scorn which kills a father's care.
  Shelley, *To the Lord Chancellor*

'You are my creator, but I am your master, - obey!'
  Shelley, *Frankenstein*

'Jekyll had more than a father's interest; Hyde had more than a son's indifference.'
  Stevenson, *Jekyll and Hyde* (also mesodiplosis)

'In manner, close and dry. In voice, husky and low.'
Dickens, *Bleak House*

'So strange in its inception and so dramatic in its details.'
Doyle, *The Engineer's Thumb*

Contrasted Bicolon

'I was required to exchange chimeras of boundless grandeur for realities of little worth.'
Shelley, *Frankenstein*

'I very well know that I am a weak, light, girlish creature, and that he is a firm, grave, serious man.'
Dickens, *David Copperfield*

'He looked for judgement, but beheld oppression; for righteousness, but beheld a cry.' (also ellipsis)
Buchan, *Witch Wood*

'The death of night, rather than the birth of day.'
Dickens, *Oliver Twist*

'A man who knows the price of everything and the value of nothing.'
Wilde, *Lady Windermere's Fan*

'Mars by day, Apollo by night. Bang the field piece, twang the lyre.'
Dickens, *The Pickwick Papers*

'The strong do what they can and the weak suffer what they must.'
Thucydides

TRICOLON
(TRI coh lon)
Balanced structure in three successive phrases

In writing and rhetoric there is a rule of three, which gives a natural sense of completeness. Examples can range from Caesar's, 'Veni, vidi, vici' - 'I came, I saw, I conquered' to hackneyed merisms like, 'lock, stock and barrel', 'Tom, Dick and Harry' or the three virtues, 'faith, hope and charity'. Some tricolons are equally balanced whilst others use the first two parts as stepping stones towards a climax or to build expectation before a twist on the third.

Balanced Tricolon

'War is peace. Freedom is slavery. Ignorance is strength.'
Orwell, *Nineteen Eighty-Four*

'It was reckless without hardihood, greedy without audacity, and cruel without courage.'
Conrad, *Heart of Darkness*

'It is a remarkable example of the confusion into which the present age has fallen; of the obliteration of landmarks, the opening of floodgates, and the uprooting of distinctions.'
Dickens, *Bleak House*

'There will be no loyalty except loyalty towards the Party. There will be no love, except the love of Big Brother. There will be no laughter, except the laugh of triumph over a defeated enemy.' (also anaphora)
Orwell, *Nineteen Eighty-Four*

'The Vincys had the readiness to enjoy, the rejection of all anxiety, and the belief in life as a merry lot.'
Eliot, *Middlemarch*

'The excellent old gentleman's nails are long and leaden, and his hands are lean and veinous, and his eyes green and watery.'
Dickens, *Bleak House*

'Revenge never worries my heart, degradation never too deeply disgusts me, injustice never crushes me too low.'
Brontë, *Jane Eyre*

'Friends, Romans, countrymen, lend me your ears.'
Shakespeare, *Julius Caesar*

Tricolon with a Twist

Another useful function of tricolon is to use the first two units as stepping stones or to set a pattern before introducing an unexpected third unit. Examples can be found in common phrases such as 'lies, damned lies, and statistics'.

> 'You can fool some of the people all of the time, and all of the people some of the time, but you cannot fool all of the people all of the time.'
> Abraham Lincoln

> 'It was bad, it was bad, it was infinitely bad!'
> Woolf, *To the Lighthouse*

> 'Great minds discuss ideas. Average minds discuss events. Small minds discuss people.'
> Eleanor Roosevelt

> 'Tell me and I forget. Teach me and I may remember. Involve me and I will learn.'
> Benjamin Franklin

> 'I require three things in a man. He must be handsome, ruthless, and stupid.'
> Dorothy Parker

POLYSYNDETON
(pol ee SIN deh ton)
Repeated use of a conjunction

Polysyndeton is a scheme of repetition in which a number of consecutive words or phrases are connected by the same repeated conjunction:

> When you are old and gray and full of sleep,
> And nodding by the fire, take down this book
> And slowly read, and dream of the soft look
> Your eyes had once, and of their shadows deep
> Yeats, *When You are Old*

In another example of polysyndeton, Shakespeare uses the device to fit iambic pentameter:

> 'Sith I have cause and will and strength and means.'
> Shakespeare, *Hamlet*

Polysyndeton can present lists of subjects or ideas as monotonous, overwhelming or just plain busy. It can be used to link steps towards a climax or anti-climax or even to signify a passage of time. However, writers should use this scheme carefully as it can, in the wrong hands, easily produce childish sounding prose.

By far the most commonly used conjunction in polysyndeton is 'and', but 'or' and 'nor' are also frequent.

Polysyndeton using 'and':

> 'Mr Copperfield was very kind to me and took a great deal of notice of me, and paid me a good deal of attention, and at last proposed to me. And I accepted him. And so we were married.'
> Dickens, *David Copperfield*

> 'Twelve struck, and one, and two, and three, and still we sat waiting silently for whatever might befall.'
> Doyle, *The Speckled Band*

Polysyndeton using 'or':

> And find him; by the happy threshold, he
> Or hand in hand with Plenty in the maize
> Or red with spirted purple of the vats,
> Or foxlike in the vine
> Tennyson, *Come Down, O Maid*

> SATAN What Vice?
> PUG   Why, any: Fraud, Or Covetousness, or Lady Vanity, Or old Iniquity.
> Marlowe, *The Jew of Malta*

> 'As mine own face. If there be cords, or knives, Poison, or fire, or suffocating streams, /I'll not endure it.'
> Shakespeare, *Othello*

Polysyndeton using 'nor':

> Such as nor voice, nor lute, nor wind, nor bird
> The soul ever stirred.
> > Shelley, *Aziola*

> 'What's Montague? it is nor hand, nor foot,
> Nor arm, nor face, nor any other part
> Belonging to a man.'
> > Shakespeare, *Romeo and Juliet*

> No birth, identity, form—no object of the world.
> Nor life, nor force, nor any visible thing;
> > Whitman, *Continuities*

ASYNDETON
(ay SIN deh ton)
Omission of conjunctions

Asyndeton is a scheme in which all conjunctions are omitted between clauses. Perhaps the best known historical example is Caesar's, 'I came. I saw. I conquered.' Each of these statements could be interspersed with a variety of conjunctions but the brevity of asyndeton ensures impact and power. It can also be used to present emotive, broken lists of ideas or to simulate a character's train of thought:

> 'He wants that key. It's mine, I paid the rent. Now I eat his salt bread. Give him the key too. All. He will ask for it. That was in his eyes.'
> > Joyce, *Ulysses*

> 'Camp, cook, sleep, strike camp, march.'
> > Conrad, *Heart of Darkness*

> 'Hackney cars, cabs, delivery waggons, mailvans, private broughams, aerated mineral water floats with rattling crates of bottles, rattled, rolled, horsedrawn, rapidly.'
> > Joyce, *Ulysses*

'Are all thy conquests, glories, triumphs, spoils,
Shrunk to this little measure?'
    Shakespeare, *Julius Caesar*

PARATAXIS
(pah rah TAK sis)
Clauses without subordination

Parataxis is a scheme in which clauses are arranged without subordination. It produces a clipped, abrupt style of writing in the same way as asyndeton but may also include coordinating conjunctions:

'The horses were put in - the driver mounted - the fat boy clambered up by his side - farewells were exchanged - and the carriage rattled off.'
    Dickens, *The Pickwick Papers*

'It was a bright cold day in April, and the clocks were striking thirteen.'
    Orwell, *Nineteen Eighty-Four*

'It makes him, and it mars him; it sets him on, and it takes him off; it persuades him, and disheartens him.'
    Shakespeare, *Macbeth*

'And what is death, he asked, your mother's or yours or my own? You saw only your mother die. I see them pop off every day in the Mater and Richmond and cut up into tripes in the dissecting room. It's a beastly thing and nothing else. It simply doesn't matter.'
    Joyce, *Ulysses*

HYPOTAXIS
(hi poh TAK sis)
Clauses with subordination

Hypotaxis differs from parataxis by its use of subordination. It establishes relationships between clauses, making some dependent on others, thus creating much more complicated sentences.

> 'He thought it with a kind of sadness, although well knowing that Syme despised him and slightly disliked him, and was fully capable of denouncing him as a thought-criminal if he saw any reason for doing so.'
> Orwell, *Nineteen Eighty-Four*

Four Figures of Conjunction

The four related figures, hypotaxis, parataxis, polysyndeton and asyndeton, can be best exemplified by showing how a sentence can be transposed through each of them:

Hypotaxis (using subordinating conjunctions)
'As soon as I finished work, I hopped onto the bus and went straight to the pet shop because I wanted to buy a new tortoise and take it home.'

Parataxis (coordinating conjunctions, no subordinating)
'I finished work. I hopped onto the bus and went straight to the pet shop. I wanted to buy a new tortoise and take it home.'

Polysyndeton (repeating the same conjunction many times)
'I wanted to buy a new tortoise and take it home and I finished work and I hopped onto the bus and went straight to the pet shop.'

Asyndeton (no conjunctions)
'I finished work. Hopped onto the bus. Went straight to the pet shop. I wanted to buy a new tortoise. To take it home.'

Figures of Disruption

Hyperbaton, Hypallage, Hendiadys, Anthimeria, Tmesis

HYPERBATON
(hi PER bah ton)
Departure from normal word order

Hyperbaton is a figure in which subjects, verbs and objects of sentences are presented in an unusual order. In a much wider sense hyperbaton includes all disruptive schemes such as hypallage, hendiadys, anthimeria and tmesis. However, these are all explained in detail in separate entries. Hyperbaton can be found throughout literature - or to put it another way - found throughout literature, hyperbaton can be:

'Some rise by sin, and some by virtue fall.'
　　Shakespeare, *Measure for Measure*

'But pleasures are like poppies spread.'
　　Burns, *Tam O'Shanter*

Stone Walls do not a Prison make,
Nor Iron bars a Cage;
Minds innocent and quiet take
That for an Hermitage
　　Lovelace, *To Althea, from Prison*

'Home also I cannot go.'
　　Joyce, *Ulysses*

'Bloody thou art; bloody will be thy end.'
　　Shakespeare, *Richard III* (also anaphora)

'Object there was none. Passion there was none.'
　　Poe, *The Tell-Tale Heart* (also epiphora)

'Waiters never walk or run. They have a peculiar and mysterious power of skimming out of rooms, which other mortals possess not.'
　　Dickens, *The Pickwick Papers*

> 'She had borne about her for years like an arrow sticking in her heart the grief, the anguish.'
> Woolf, *Mrs Dalloway*

> 'Yet never a breeze up-blew.'
> Coleridge, *The Rime of the Ancient Mariner*

> 'Yet I'll not shed her blood;
> Nor scar that whiter skin of hers than snow.'
> Shakespeare, *Othello*

Anacoluthon (an ah coh LOO thon)

Anacoluthon is a common form of hyperbaton. This figure is employed when a character breaks off emotionally in mid-sentence, and hesitates before continuing on a different tack. These pauses are usually punctuated by ellipsis marks '…' or dashes.

> 'No, you unnatural hags, I will have such revenges on you both, That all the world shall--I will do such things,-- What they are, yet I know not.'
> Shakespeare, *King Lear*

> 'I know him to be Mr. Quinion, whom I had gone over to Lowestoft with Mr Murdstone to see, before - it is no matter - I need not recall when.'
> Dickens, *David Copperfield*

> 'Between the tall rhododendrons and the conifers, before the lodge became visible, he inclined his face towards her as if - but, no!'
> Hardy, *Tess of the d'Urbervilles*

In this final example the narrator hesitates rather than a character. (see ellipsis, apostrophe)

HYPALLAGE
(hi PAL ah jay)
Epithet transferred to an inappropriate noun

Hypallage is a figure in which a word, usually an adjective, is transferred to an inappropriate position to modify another word, hence its alternative name - transferred epithet. It is quite common in phrases such as 'a sad day', 'uncomfortable shoes', 'happy journey'.

On occasion, the resulting misapplied attribution of emotions to inanimate objects can be erroneously categorised as personification. For example, in Wilfred Owen's *Dulce et Decorum Est.*, the poet describes soldiers amid the slaughter of the First World War 'fitting the clumsy helmets just in time'; obviously, Owen did not decide to insert a whimsical personification of a helmet amid the carnage; the soldiers are the ones whom the adjective describes. This is a perfect example of hypallage: the young men are so clumsy that the epithet is shifted to the wrong place in the sentence thus heightening the sense of panic.

Hypallage can be used to modify just about anything from anatomy to abstractions:

Hypallage of anatomy:

'I had been permitted to draw back my hesitating foot.'
Conrad, *Heart of Darkness*

'She turned an indifferent ear to the compliments with which she was addressed.'
Scott, *Old Mortality*

'A red-haired man with an inquisitive nose and blue spectacles.'
Dickens, *The Pickwick Papers*

'Most absurd gratification of a misjudging eye.'
Smollett, *The Expedition of Humphry Clinker*

'Wrinkling a contumelious nostril, as usual, at the Italian renaissance sculpture.'
O Henry, *Mammon and the Archer*

Hypallage of objects:

'I would recommend a hasty sandwich.'
Dickens, *Bleak House*

'Now do those two gentlemen… dive into the Sol's
parlour, and write with ravenous little pens.'
   Dickens, *Bleak House*

'A large room… rising on clumsy Saxon pillars.'
   Scott, *Ivanhoe*

'And never brandish more revengeful steel
Over the glittering helmet of my foe!'
   Shakespeare, *Richard II*

'Our Italy / Shines o'er with civil swords.'
   Shakespeare, *Anthony and Cleopatra*

'His linen is arranged to a nicety, and he is wrapped in a
responsible dressing-gown.'
   Dickens, *Bleak House*

'And by the happy hollow of a tree / Escap'd the hunt.'
   Shakespeare, *King Lear*

Hypallage of weather:

'The rain happily stopped, and I prepared for our walk.'
   James, *The Turn of the Screw*

'In the whole length of the single shoreside street, with
its scattered board houses looking to the sea, its grateful
shade of palms and green jungle puraos, no moving
figure could be seen.'
   Stevenson, *The Wrecker*

In the following example, the first hypallage is an abstraction and
the second an object:

'O, most wicked speed, to post
With such dexterity to incestuous sheets!'
   Shakespeare, *Hamlet*

HENDIADYS
(hen DIE ah dis)
Adjective and noun as two nouns

Hendiadys is a scheme in which a single idea is divided in two. A pair of normally consecutive words are separated and reassembled using a conjunction. When Lady Macbeth asks:

'Art thou afeard to be the same in thine own act and valour as thou art in desire?'
Shakespeare, *Macbeth*

Shakespeare uses 'act and valour' instead of 'valorous act'; two nouns are presented rather than a noun and a modifying adjective. The scheme works by eliminating the inferior-superior relationship and leaving the two words in balance.

'We heard the angry cries.' - 'We heard the cries and anger.'

'His humbly contrite spirit.' - 'His humble and contrite spirit.'

The first of these examples changes adjective to noun and the second, adverb to adjective. Most examples of this figure are found in the works of Shakespeare:

Adjective - noun:

'It is a tale / Told by an idiot, full of sound and fury.'
Shakespeare, *Macbeth*

'The heaviness and guilt within my bosom takes off my manhood.'
Shakespeare, *Cymbeline*

'But faintly, nothing like the image / and horror of it.'
Shakespeare, *King Lear*

'It harrows me with fear and wonder.'
Shakespeare, *Hamlet*

'To their lord's murder: roasted in wrath and fire.'
Shakespeare, *Hamlet*

Adverb - adjective:

'The single and peculiar life is bound.'
Shakespeare, *Hamlet*

'These are but wild and whirling words, my lord.'
Shakespeare, *Hamlet*

'Th' extravagant and erring spirit hies / To his confine.'
Shakespeare, *Hamlet*

ANTHIMERIA
(an thi MEE ree ah)
Using one part of speech in place of another

When someone says 'my bad' rather than 'my mistake' or that they can't just 'magic' something out of thin air, rather than 'conjure', they are using an adjective for a noun and a noun for a verb respectively. This is anthimeria. It may, at first, seem like bad grammar and can, if truth be told, be the cause of much inane management speak: 'Do we have a solve for this?', 'Can you action that?' Nonetheless, many great lines have been 'penned' using this device.

In *Hamlet*, Shakespeare's eponymous hero is angry with his mother and declares, 'I will speak daggers to her but use none'; he means that he will speak harshly or angrily and his words will be metaphorically cutting. This is brought into much sharper focus by using a noun rather than an adverb.

Various parts of speech can be exchanged:

'They've got a gallows bad reputation.'
Stevenson, *The Beach of Falesá*

'He looked encyclopaedias at Mr Peter Magnus.'
Dickens, *The Pickwick Papers*

'The old lady… drew herself up, and looked carving-knives at the hard-headed delinquent.'
Dickens, *The Pickwick Papers*

One form of anthimeria uses a noun for a verb and is also known as 'verbification'. 'To text' and 'to email' are recent examples.

> 'It was good to foot the grass.'
> Stevenson, *The Beach of Falesá*

> 'A mile before his tent fall down, and knee
> The way into his mercy.'
> Shakespeare, *Coriolanus*

> 'Here have I purs'd their paltry silverlings.'
> Marlowe, *The Jew of Malta*

Another form of anthimeria is used to reflect and respond to a word uttered by another character. It presents the noun as a verb, followed by 'me no', then the original noun as plural, thus creating a kind of polyptoton:

> His party, cried "Advance and take thy prize
> The diamond;" but he answered, "Diamond me
> No diamonds! for God's love, a little air!
> Prize me no prizes, for my prize is death!"
> Tennyson, *Lancelot and Elaine*

> 'Grace me no grace, nor uncle me no uncle.'
> Shakespeare, *Richard II*

> 'Thank me no thankings, nor, proud me no prouds.'
> Shakespeare, *Romeo and Juliet*

> 'Clerk me no clerks.'
> Scott, *Ivanhoe*

> 'Character me no characters.'
> Hogg, *The Three Perils of Ma*n

> 'But Flaubert me no Flauberts, Bovary me no Bovarys. Zola me no Zolas. And exuberance me no exuberances.'
> Thomas Wolfe

TMESIS
(ti MEE sis)
Splitting a word

Tmesis is a disruptive figure in which a word is split and, more often than not, has another word inserted in the resulting space. It is a useful way of bringing attention to the word by breaking it into constituent parts and highlighting it even more with the unexpected, often vulgar, insertion. The expletives can vary from the whimsical to the taboo. Neverthe-bloody-less, I can guaran-damn-tee that it's fan-bloomin-tastic.

Splitting
The most basic timetic form simply splits the word and inserts a space to create a slight pause for emphasis, as in 'Im-possible'.

'And the profits, I am told, are e-NOR-mous.'
Dickens, *David Copperfield*

'Ex-act-ly - pre-cise-ly: with your usual acuteness, you have hit the nail on the head.'
Brontë, *Jane Eyre*

Insertion
The best known form of tmesis has a word or phrase inserted in the space. A wide variety of words can be used, although in everyday speech these are mainly expletives. Any-old-how, here are a few literary examples:

'This is not Romeo; he is some other where.'
Shakespeare, *Romeo and Juliet*

Whatseasoever swallow me, that flood
Shall be to me an emblem of thy blood.
Donne, *Hymn to Christ*

'A whole 'nother day in the house and in the dark.'
Molesworth, *The Story of a Spring Morning*

'That man – how dearly ever parted.'
Shakespeare, *Troilus and Cressida*

'If on the first, how heinous e'er it be.'
　　Shakespeare, *Richard II*

Creating Tmeses

The construction of tmeses is rather simple. Firstly, choose any word with two or more syllables that does not have stress on its first syllable. For instance, 'macaroni' or 'elementary' rather than 'caterpillar' or 'dictionary'. Then split the word immediately before the stressed syllable: 'maca / roni', 'ele / mentary'. Next simply put any word in the space: 'maca-bloomin-roni', 'ele-diddly-mentary'. Choosing this position for the split engages the natural pronunciation of the word to give more power to the disruption. There is, of course, one exception: prefixed words are best interrupted between the first and second syllables: 'un-bloody-believable'.

Figures of Omission and Sharing
Ellipsis, Zeugma, Syllepsis, Diazeugma

A note on Ellipsis, Zeugma and Syllepsis

These three schemes are often confused and many textbooks and dictionaries disagree on exactly which does what.

Ellipsis means to omit a word and zeugma to share one. As in the preceding sentence, a verb is sometimes omitted to avoid unnecessary repetition. For example: 'Billy enjoyed a beer and Florence a cocktail'; it could be argued that, because the verb 'enjoyed' is now being shared, this should be categorised as zeugma rather than ellipsis. However, if we compare this simple sharing with the discordant sharing of true zeugma: 'Billy enjoyed a beer and his memories'; in this sentence the two objects mismatch; one is concrete and the other is abstract. By using this device, the author can produce a little literary magic. Therefore, zeugma is better reserved for this discordant kind of sharing and ellipsis for omission. Syllepsis is often presented as nothing more than a synonym of zeugma. However, it can be defined more precisely as a figure in which the shared word causes a grammatical error whereas zuegma merely produces clever discordance.

In an attempt to clarify things, the table below presents the figures of omission and sharing in three distinct ways:

Figures of Sharing

Ellipsis	Duplicated verb omitted leaving harmonious nouns	'She went to the library and he the casino.'
Zeugma	Word shared with discordant objects	'She was looking for a new book and a divorce.'
Syllepsis	Word shared that causes problems grammatically	'She took the book and up karate.' 'The king rules the castle but the people the streets.'

ELLIPSIS
(eh LIP sis)
Omission of words easily understood

Ellipsis is a figure in which a word or words are omitted but are still understood. This can either be because the missing words are easily inferred, to avoid unnecessary repetition or because of a character's awkwardness or inability to continue.

Ellipsis of Words Easily Inferred

There are a multitude of reasons to omit words from texts. In the first of the following examples, Shakespeare uses ellipsis to preserve iambic pentameter, in the second, Joyce's character omits a word out of politeness, but in each case the missing word is understood:

'And he to England shall along with you.'
    Shakespeare, *Hamlet*

"Did he… peacefully?" she asked.
    Joyce, *Dubliners*

'Desire them home.'
    Shakespeare, *Troilus and Cressida*

'Haply you shall not see me more, or if,
A mangled shadow.'
    Shakespeare, *Anthony and Cleopatra*

Ellipsis of Unnecessary Repetition

This form of ellipsis omits words or phrases that have already been used and in the sentence. (sometimes classed as zeugma)

'I neither know it nor can learn of him'
    Shakespeare, *Romeo and Juliet*

'Try not to associate bodily defects with mental.'
    Dickens, *David Copperfield*

'She had no need to say a word. Mr Peggoty understood her quite as well as if she had said a thousand.'
    Dickens, *David Copperfield*

'All women become like their mothers. That is their
tragedy. No man does. That's his.'
    Oscar Wilde

The lightest wind was in its nest
The tempest in its home.
    Shelley, *To Jane*

Give them thy fingers, me thy lips to kiss.
    Shakespeare, *Sonnet CXXVIII*

'Some cause happiness wherever they go; others
whenever they go.'
    Oscar Wilde

'The work appears to be light, and the pay munificent.'
    Doyle, *The Engineer's Thumb*

'Her sorrows were known to man; her virtues to God.'
    Dickens, *The Pickwick Papers*

Trailing Ellipsis

In another form, ellipsis indicates a character hesitating in mid-sentence and trailing off due to awkwardness or heightened emotion. The three punctuation points '…' or occasionally dashes used to indicate missing words are known as ellipsis marks. This form differs from the previous examples inasmuch as the missing words are less obvious and are left to the imagination of the reader.

' "She'll think of me as an incarnate insult to her, from
the first moment we…"
Will stopped as if he had found himself grasping
something that must not be thrown and shattered.'
    Eliot, *Middlemarch*

"You couldn't tell when the breath went out of him. He
had a beautiful death, God be praised."
"And everything… ?"
"Father O'Rourke was in with him a Tuesday and
anointed him and prepared him and all."
    Joyce, *Dubliners*

"As for you, you'd forget me."
"That I never should, sir: you know - "
Brontë, *Jane Eyre*

This form of ellipsis is related to another two common figures-

Trailing Ellipsis	Character stops mid-sentence.
Anacoluthon	Character stops and changes the subject.
Apostrophe	Appeals to a deity or someone not present.

ZEUGMA
(ZOOG ma)
Sharing a word with discordant results

Zeugma is a scheme in which a word, usually a verb, is shared in an discordant way. Although the resulting sentence is grammatically correct, the shared word modifies the others in different ways. For example:

And the waves oozing through the port-hole made
His berth a little damp, and him afraid.
Byron, *Don Juan*

In Byron's example the verb 'made' has a different effect on 'his berth' and 'him'. The zeugmatic effect is thus achieved by linking a verb or other part of speech with incompatible nouns to produce a discordant result that has to be reconciled by the reader. This is well exemplified when Mark Twain describes the young boys' fighting:

'They tugged and tore at each other's hair and clothes,
punched and scratched each other's nose, and covered
themselves with dust and glory.'
Twain, *Tom Sawyer*

Here, 'dust' is a concrete noun and 'glory' is abstract, but both are served by the same verb, 'covered'.

Zeugma of various parts of speech
Most zeugmas are verbs but often use other parts of speech:

Zeugma of Verbs:

Or stain her honour, or her new brocade,
Forget her pray'rs, or miss a masquerade;
Or lose her heart, or necklace, at a ball;
Or whether Heav'n has doom'd that Shock must fall.
   Pope, *The Rape of the Lock*

The loud tempests raise
The waters, and repentance for past sinning.
   Byron, *Don Juan*

'Alternating from week to week between cocaine and ambition.'
   Doyle, *A Scandal in Bohemia*

'He usually sat at one of Tildy's tables and devoted himself to silence and boiled weakfish.'
   O Henry, *The Brief Debut of Tildy*

'He had increased as well in purse as in corpulence.'
   Scott, *Old Mortality*

'The laity sometimes suffer in peace and pocket.'
   Dickens, *Bleak House*

Zeugma of Adjectives:

'He passed out with grave words and gait.'
   Joyce, *Ulysses*

'London is too full of fogs and serious people.'
   Wilde, *Lady Windermere's Fan*

Zeugma of Prepositions:

'Miss Bolo rose from the table considerably agitated, and went straight home, in a flood of tears, and a sedan chair.'
   Dickens, *The Pickwick Papers*

Zeugmatic Forms

In most of the preceding examples, the shared word comes before the nouns; this is more accurately known as prozeugma. If the shared word appears between nouns it is known as mezozeugma and after, hypozeugma.

Prozeugma:

> 'He struck off his pension and his head together.'
> Dickens, *The Pickwick Papers*

Mezozuegma:

> Here thou, great Anna! whom three realms obey
> Dost sometimes counsel take - and sometimes tea.
> Pope, *The Rape of the Lock*

> 'At last, when the punch was all gone, and the night nearly so.'
> Dickens, *The Pickwick Papers*

Hypozuegma:

> 'Yet time and her aunt moved slowly.'
> Austen, *Pride and Prejudice*

Hypozeuxis:

Hypozeuxis is a figure in which every phrase has its own subject and verb. Nothing is shared and it could therefore be described as the opposite of zeugma.

> 'Madam, the guests are come, supper served up, you called, my young lady asked for, the nurse cursed in the pantry, and every thing in extremity.'
> Shakespeare, *Romeo and Juliet*

> 'The dogs barked, the mob screamed, the troops recovered.'
> Dickens, *The Pickwick Papers*

SYLLEPSIS
(sih LEP sis)
Sharing a word causes grammatical error

Syllepsis is another form of sharing, but differs from zeugma inasmuch as the verb being shared is grammatically incompatible with at least one of the desired objects. For example:

'As you on him, Demetrius dote on you.'
Shakespeare's, *A Midsummer Night's Dream*

The verb 'dote' is being shared but does not agree with both 'you' and 'Demetrius'. The same kind of error can be seen in the following examples:

'She has deceiv'd her father, and may thee.'
Shakespeare, *Othello*

'He works his work, I mine.'
Tennyson, *Ulysses*

'My ladie laughs for joy, and I for woe.'
Puttenham, *The Arte of English Poesie*

Phrasal Verb Syllepsis

Syllepsis also refers to the combination of phrasal and plain verbs when the phrasal verb is split. For example, 'to fall' is a plain verb whereas to 'to fall out' is a phrasal verb. These can then be combined sylleptically by splitting the phrasal verb: 'He fell from grace and out with his mother', 'They made pizza and up with each other'.

DIAZEUGMA
(die ah ZOOG ma)
Sharing a subject with many verbs

Whereas zeugma primarily means to share a number of nouns with a single verb, diazeugma shares a number of verbs with a single subject. This scheme is an excellent way of controlling pace. The first of the following examples by Dickens, crams the events together creating a sense of rapidity and the second slows things down as Bumble is preparing to speak.

'Mr Bob Sawyer pushed the postboy on one side, jerked his friend into the vehicle, slammed the door, put up the steps, wafered the bill on the street door, locked it, put the key in his pocket, jumped into the dickey, gave the word for starting, and did the whole with such extraordinary precipitation, that before Mr. Pickwick had well begun to consider whether Mr. Bob Sawyer ought to go or not, they were rolling away, with Mr. Bob Sawyer thoroughly established as part and parcel of the equipage.'
Dickens, *The Pickwick Papers*

'Mr Bumble put down his hat; unbuttoned his coat; folded his arms; inclined his head in a retrospective manner; and, after a few moments' reflection, commenced his story.'
Dickens, *Oliver Twist*

'Thou wert born amongst rocks, suckled by whales, cradled in a tempest, and whistled to by winds.'
Congreve, *Love for Love*

'She enters into her scheme of economy, learns her phrases, repeats her remarks, imitates her stile (sic) in scolding the inferior servants, and, finally, subscribes implicitly to her system of devotion.'
Smollett, *The Expedition of Humphry Clinker*

'He was pinched in, and swelled out, and got up, and strapped down.'
Dickens, *Bleak House*

Figures of Sound

Most of these figures involve repetition. However, this is based on repeated sounds rather than words. Consonance and assonance encompass the majority of matching sounds, but it can be seen how alliteration is closely related to anaphora, with epiphora and rhyme having a similar relationship. On the other hand, dissonance is employed to disrupt the melodic flow whilst onomatopoeia mimics both sound and movement.

Repeated Sounds

Consonance, Alliteration, Sibilance, Assonance, Rhyme

CONSONANCE
(CON soh nans)
Repeated arranged consonants

Consonance has two forms. In the strictest of these, 'perfect' consonance, a sequence of consonantal sounds is repeated with a change in intervening vowels, as in 'tick tock', 'digger dagger', 'crack croak'. The second, much simpler form, known as 'imperfect' consonance, is found when unpaired stressed consonant sounds are repeated. (If stressed sounds are located mainly at the beginnings of nearby words, it may be categorised as alliteration which is a branch of consonance.)

Perfect Consonance

'The vorpal blade went snicker-snack!'
    Carroll, *Jabberwocky*

I am the enemy you killed, my friend.
I knew you in this dark: for so you frowned
Yesterday through me as you jabbed and killed.
I parried; but my hands were loath and cold.
    Owen, *Strange Meeting*

'Disease in general was called by some bad name, and treated accordingly without shilly-shally.'
    Eliot, *Middlemarch*

Imperfect Consonance

The grey sea and the long black land;
And the yellow half-moon large and low;
And the startled little waves that leap
In fiery ringlets from their sleep,
    Browning, *Meeting at Night*

The moan of doves in immemorial elms
And murmuring of innumerable bees
    Tennyson, *Come Down, O Maid*

Moses, from whose loins I sprung,
Lit by a lamp in his blood
Ten immutable rules, a moon
For mutable lampless men.
    Rosenberg, *The Jew*

ALLITERATION
(ah lih ter AY shon)
Repetition of initial stressed consonants

    Alliteration is a figure in which consonantal sounds are repeated mainly at the beginnings of nearby words. It is extremely popular in idiomatic speech and stock similes: 'cool as a cucumber', 'gas guzzler', 'labour of love' or from Dickens' *A Christmas Carol*: 'Old Marley was as dead as a door-nail.' Alliteration can also be used to give a sense of completion to lists and extremes: 'dawn till dusk', 'right and wrong', 'from Birmingham to Bangladesh'. The repeated consonant sounds primarily begin words but can also be matched with other stressed syllables:

'It flows purling, widely flowing floating foampool,
flower unfurling.'
    Joyce, *Ulysses*

    It should be noted that alliteration refers only to consonants despite regularly and erroneously being used for vowel sounds and sibilants, which are, more precisely, assonance and sibilance. Another important point is that alliteration is not based on spelling but sound, as with the 'qu' and the hard 'c' in this example:

'Over many a quaint and curious volume of forgotten lore.'
    Poe, *The Raven*

    Names of superheroes and their enemies are commonly alliterative: 'Bruce Banner', 'Peter Parker', 'Clark Kent', 'Lex

Luthor' and of course, 'Postman Pat'. Many famous novels also have alliterative titles:

The Great Gatsby - F. Scott Fitzgerald

Pride and Prejudice - Jane Austen

A Tale of Two Cities - Charles Dickens

Peter Pan - J. M. Barrie

Brighton Rock - Graham Greene

Rob Roy - Walter Scott

Witch Wood - John Buchan

Alliteration in Poetry:

Bore up his branching head; scarce from his mould
Behemoth, biggest born of earth, upheaved
    Milton, *Paradise Lost*

The fair breeze blew, the white foam flew,
The furrow followed free
    Coleridge, *The Rime of the Ancient Mariner*

'Nae man can tether time or tide.'
    Burns, *Tam O'Shanter*

'Only the stuttering rifles' rapid rattle.'
    Owen, *Anthem for Doomed Youth*

'The woodman winding westward up the glen.'
    Coleridge, *Constancy to an Ideal Object*

Alliteration in Prose:

'There is something wrong with his appearance; something displeasing, something downright detestable.'
    Stevenson, *Jekyll and Hyde*

'Hoover, forty-five, flush, foolish and fat.'
    O Henry, *The Skylight Room*

'Proud people breed sad sorrows for themselves.' (also sibilance)
  Brontë, *Wuthering Heights*

'Anonymous libels, letters and lampoons.'
  Smollett, *The Expedition of Humphry Clinker*

Paroemion

Paroemion is an old term for alliteration which is now used pejoratively to describe excessive use of the device. It can be seen at work in the following examples, firstly by Shakespeare to highlight some overenthusiastic alliteration in the 'play within the play' and secondly by Dickens to make the many parts of an election process appear ridiculous:

'Whereat, with blade, with bloody, blameful blade
He bravely broach'd his boiling bloody breast.'
  Shakespeare, *A Midsummer Night's Dream*

'A quantity of printing, and promising, and proxying, and polling.'
  Dickens, *Bleak House*

SIBILANCE
(SIH bih lans)
Repeated sibilant sounds

Sibilance is a branch of consonance in which fricative sounds are repeated in nearby words. The main fricatives are 's', 'sh', 'ch' and 'z': 'sixteen silly snakes', 'she washes shrimps', 'the chimp chopped branches on the beach', 'zebras are always amazing'.

Sibilance - S:

Deals out that being indoors each one dwells;
Selves — goes itself; myself it speaks and spells,
  Hopkins, *As Kingfishers Catch Fire*

'Secrets, silent, stony sit in the dark palaces of both our hearts.'
  Joyce, *Ulysses*

'To sit a star upon the sparkling spire.'
   Tennyson, *The Princess*

'Softly drank through his straight gums, into his slack long body / Silently.'
   Lawrence, *Snake*

'The serpent hisses where the sweet bird sings.'
   Hardy, *Tess of the d'Urbervilles*

Where thoughts serenely sweet express
   Byron, *She Walks in Beauty*

And men, despairing in deathly queues,
Heard their own heart-beats
Shouting aloud in the silence of the streets
   Soutar, *The Guns*

Sibilance - Sh:

But how shall finished creatures
A function fresh obtain?
   Dickinson, *The Bone that has no Marrow*

'That I will show you shining at this feast,
And she shall scant show well that now shows best.'
   Shakespeare, *Romeo and Juliet*

'I shall no more to sea, to sea,
Here shall I die ashore.'
   Shakespeare, *The Tempest*

Within the shadow of the ship
I watched their rich attire
   Coleridge, *Rime of the Ancient Mariner*

Sibilance - Ch:

Within my reach!
I could have touched!
I might have chanced that way!
   Dickinson, *Almost!*

'O, she doth teach the torches to burn bright!
It seems she hangs upon the cheek of night
Like a rich jewel in an Ethiope's ear;
Beauty too rich for use, for earth too dear!'
    Shakespeare, *Romeo and Juliet*

The charms o' the min', the langer they shine,
The mair admiration they draw, man;
While peaches and cherries, and roses and lilies,
They fade and they wither awa, man
    Burns, *Ronalds Of The Bennals*

Sibilance - Z:

A bow-shot from her bower-eaves,
He rode between the barley sheaves,
The sun came dazzling thro' the leaves,
And flamed upon the brazen greaves
    Tennyson, *The Lady of Shallot*

'Men's eyes were made to look, and let them gaze.'
    Shakespeare, *Romeo and Juliet*

ASSONANCE
(ASS oh nans)
Repetition of stressed vowels

Whether you are 'down and out' or 'happy as Larry', a 'good woman' or a 'bad man', a 'young buck' or a 'coffin dodger', you are also an excellent example of assonance. Closely related to rhyme, this is a device in which stressed vowel sounds are repeated primarily without matching consonants. As it concerns only vowel sounds, it is a counterpart to consonance. Assonant sounds may occur at beginnings of words - 'Aberdeen Angus', in the middle - 'the squeaky wheel gets the grease', or at the end - 'fade to grey' where it creates assonant rhyme.

When I have fears that I may cease to be
Before my pen has gleaned my teeming brain
    Keats, *When I have Fears that I may Cease to Be*

'When shall we three meet again?'
   Shakespeare, *Macbeth*

'Shimmering on the dim tide.'
   Joyce, *Ulysses*

Its motion in this hush of nature
Gives it dim sympathies.
   Coleridge, *Frost at Midnight*

'A host of golden daffodils.'
   Wordsworth, *Daffodils*

'From the molten-golden notes.'
   Poe, *Bells*

When you have bid your servant once adieu.
   Shakespeare, *Sonnet LVII*

RHYME
(RIME)
Similarity of emphasised vowel sounds

Rhyme is so prevalent in poetry and music that it may seem superfluous in a guide such as this. However, there are several forms of rhyme that may be of interest to the student and writer for experiment and practice.

In its strictest form rhyme refers to the repetition of emphasised vowel sounds at ends or within lines. The consonants or consonant groups that immediately precede the vowels should also be different: 'fix - mix', 'bob - job', and 'cat - mat' are all simple rhymes, as are 'cling - bling', 'rack - track', and 'grace - trace'.

The most common forms of rhyme are categorised based on the proximity of the stressed syllable to the end of the rhymed words. Masculine, feminine and triple rhyme correspond to stress on the ultimate, penultimate and antepenultimate syllables in the words or phrases. Rhyme depends on pronunciation and rhythm rather than spelling. Therefore 'break' has no perfect rhyme with 'freak': instead, this is classed as imperfect rhyme or eye-rhyme. Rhythm is also important: 'sing' rhymes with 'cling' but neither rhyme with 'denying' because the stress falls on a different syllable.

Masculine Rhyme

In masculine rhyme, only the stressed final syllable shares its sound:

Lizzy Borden took an axe
Gave her mother forty whacks
And when she saw what she had done
She gave her father forty one
    Anon.

Then let not winter's ragged hand deface
In thee thy summer, ere thou be distill'd
Make sweet some vial; treasure thou some place
With beauty's treasure, ere it be self-kill'd
    Shakespeare, *Sonnet VI*

'Met her once in the park. In the dark. What a lark.'
    Joyce, *Ulysses*

Feminine Rhyme

In feminine rhyme, the penultimate syllable is stressed:

Look in thy glass, and tell the face thou viewest
Now is the time that face should form another;
Whose fresh repair if now thou not renewest,
Thou dost beguile the world, unbless some mother.
    Shakespeare, *Sonnet III*

'This is my grumpy, frumpy story, and we'll keep it to ourselves, Trot!'
    Dickens, *David Copperfield*

Triple Rhyme

In triple rhyme, the antepenultimate or third-last syllable is stressed. This form lends itself more to comic verse:

When you're lying awake with a dismal headache, and
repose is taboo'd by anxiety,
I conceive you may use any language you choose to
indulge in, without impropriety.
    Gilbert, *The Nightmare*

Each eye a sermon, and her brow a homily…
Like the lamented late Sir Samuel Romilly…
Whose suicide was almost an anomaly
One sad example more, that 'All is vanity'
(The jury brought their verdict in 'Insanity')
    Byron, *Don Juan*

Internal Rhyme

Words can be matched with other like-sounding words within the same line to create internal rhyme:

'We were the first that ever burst / Into that silent sea.'
    Coleridge, *The Rime of the Ancient Mariner*

They dined on mince, and slices of quince,
Which they ate with a runcible spoon;
And hand in hand, on the edge of the sand,
They danced by the light of the moon.
    Lear, *The Owl and the Pussycat*

Stones ring; like each tucked string tells, each hung bell's
Bow swung finds tongue to fling out broad its name.
    Hopkins, *As Kingfishers Catch Fire*

I never saw a purple cow,
I never hope to see one,
But I can tell you anyhow,
I'd rather see than be one.
    Burgess, *The Purple Cow*

Imperfect Rhyme

Sticking rigidly to perfect rhyme is a worthwhile challenge but can also be quite constraining. Moreover, certain perfect rhyming pairs have become worn-out over the years. Therefore, writers sometimes bend the rules a little to create imperfect rhymes. These go by a variety of names such as, assonant rhyme, near rhyme, lazy rhyme, slant rhyme etc.. As with humorous puns, the results can be cringeworthy in the wrong hands but quite often inspiring. In song lyrics, rhythm and stress are frequently altered to suit the occasion.

Discrete Sound

Dissonance, Onomatopoeia

DISSONANCE
(DIS oh nans)
A clash of sounds or rhythm

Unlike the other figures of sound in which the writer aims for harmony or euphony, when using dissonance, the intention is to create disharmony and discordance. Several clashing consonants are arranged to contrast or conflict with one another thereby making pronunciation difficult. It does not mean the complete absence of repeating figures of sound and may in fact use these for contrast with other sounds. Dissonance also refers to disruption of rhythm by using inconsistent sentence structures or breaking established meter.

> Not, I'll not, carrion comfort, Despair, not feast on thee;
> Not untwist - slack they may be - these last strands of man
> In me ór, most weary, cry I can no more. I can;
>   Hopkins, *Carrion Comfort*

> His feet on juts of slippery crag that rang
> Sharp-smitten with the dint of armed heels
>   Tennyson, *Morte D'Arthur*

> 'Twas brillig, and the slithy toves
> Did gyre and gimble in the wabe:
> All mimsy were the borogoves,
> And the mome raths outgrabe.
>   Carroll, *The Jabberwocky*

> Roll through my chant with all thy lawless music, thy swinging lamps at night,
> Thy madly-whistled laughter, echoing, rumbling like an earthquake, rousing all.
>   Whitman, *To a Locomotive in Winter*

ONOMATOPOEIA
(AWE no mah toh PEE ah)
Words imitate what they describe

Onomatopoeia is an old favourite of teachers and a rich source of creativity and amusement. In its most common guise, words closely imitate the sounds of whatever they represent, as in 'boom', 'crunch' and 'zap'. Sounds of living things are also popular and produce words like 'hiss', 'bark' and 'grunt'. However, there is also a much broader form of onomatopoeia which refers to movement using words such as 'swoosh', 'wobble' and 'stagger'.

Onomatopoeia of General Sounds

'The boom of the tingling strings.'
Lawrence, *Piano*

'Jingling and clattering.'
Dickens, *Oliver Twist*

'The occasional boom of the kettle drum… joined with the tramp of hoofs and the clash of arms, announced that the troop had resumed its march.'
Scott, *Old Mortality*

'Faint sounds rose in spirals up the well of the stairs; the swish of a mop; tapping; knocking; a loudness when the front door opened; a voice repeating a message in the basement; the chink of silver on a tray.'
Woolf, *Mrs Dalloway*

'An atmosphere of silence, haunted by the ghosts of sound - strange cracks and tickings, the rustling of garments that have no substance in them, and the tread of dreadful feet that would leave no mark.'
Dickens, *Bleak House*

'Out of this automobile comes a big blooey-blooey, with four guys letting go with sawed-off shotguns at once.'
Runyon, *Too Much Pep*

Onomatopoeia of Creature Sounds

Onomatopoeia has always been a useful device to represent sounds of animals and other wildlife. As far back as 405 BCE, in *The Frogs*, Aristophanes had his chorus repeat, 'Brekekekex, ko-ax, ko-ax Brekekekex, ko-ax, ko-ax!'

'Perhaps it is the owlet's scritch.'
Coleridge, *Cristabel*

'Alarum'd by his sentinel, the wolf,
Whose howl's his watch.'
Shakespeare, *Macbeth*

'A cock-pigeon strutted round, puffing his gleaming breast and rookety-cooing in the sun.'
Brown, *The House with the Green Shutters*

'And gathering swallows twitter in the skies.'
Keats, *To Autumn*

'And it howled in the winds, and it roared in the billows, and it screamed, and it whistled, and it clanged, with the screams and the clang and the whistle of the sea-birds as they floated and flew and dropped and dived.'
Scott, *Old Mortality*

Onomatopoeia of Movement

A less well known form of onomatopoeia refers to movement. Associated sounds can be imagined when reading these actions:

'The indefatigable birds flickered around Gretz church-tower.'
Stevenson, *Treasure of Franchard*

'John's glass shivered on his grinning teeth.'
Brown, *The House with the Green Shutters*

Like the bubbles on a river
Sparkling, bursting, borne away.
Shelley, *Hellas*

'Tumbled about among the spread nets and the glass frames sparkling and winking in the sun.'
    Dickens, *Bleak House*

'Gifts of witch-men, that hung about her, glittered and trembled at every step.'
    Conrad, *Heart of Darkness*

'The keen stars were twinkling.'
    Shelley, *To Jane*

He left it dead, and with its head
He went galumphing back.
    Carroll, *Jabberwocky*

In this final example, the reader is left to decide whether 'galumphing' is onomatopoeia of sound or of action or perhaps both.

Functional Glossary

REPEATED WORDS

Epizeuxis Immediate repetition of words **92**
Diacope Repetition of words after intervening words **94**
Anadiplosis Same words end one part and begin the next **97**
Epanalepsis Same words at beginning and end **96**
Polyptoton Words repeated in different parts of speech **99**
Antanaclasis Repeated use of homonyms **89**
Antimetabole Reflected crossover of words **102** (chiasmus)

Epizeuxis	Xxx, xxx, xxx
Diacope	…xxx…xxx…
Anadiplosis	…xxx. / Xxx…
Epanalepsis	Xxx…xxx.
Polyptoton	…xxx… (xxx)… (same root)
Antanaclasis	…xxx…xxx… (homonyms)
Antimetabole	…xxx…yyy… / …yyy…xxx…

REPEATED WORDS OR PHRASES

Anaphora Repetition of beginnings of consecutive word units **104**
Epiphora Repetition of endings of consecutive word units **107**
Symploce Repetition of both anaphora and epiphora **108**
Mesodiplosis Repetition of middles of consecutive word units **110**

Anaphora	Xxx…/ Xxx…
Epiphora	…yyy. / …yyy.
Symploce	Xxx…yyy. / Xxx…yyy.
Mesodiplosis	…xxx… / …xxx…

STRUCTURE AND RELATION OF WORD UNITS
Bicolon Balanced structure in two consecutive word units **114**
Tricolon Balanced structure in three consecutive word units **115**
Isocolon Balanced structure in several consecutive word units **112**
Antithesis Contrast of ideas in balanced phrases **85**
Chiasmus Reflected crossover of meaning in phrases **101**
Hypotaxis Sequence of sentences with subordination **121**
Parataxis Sequence of sentences without subordination **120**
Polysyndeton Sequence with same repeated conjunction **117**
Asyndeton Omission of all conjunctions **119**

Bicolon	Unit, Unit
Tricolon	Unit, Unit, Unit
Isocolon	Unit, Unit, Unit, Unit…
Antithesis	Unit / Unit (opposite)
Chiasmus	Unit A…Unit B, Unit B2…Unit A2
Hypotaxis	Unit and unit because unit
Parataxis	Unit and unit (no subordination)
Polysyndeton	Unit and unit and unit and unit
Asyndeton	Unit. Unit. Unit.

SHARING OR OMITTING WORDS
Asyndeton Omission of all conjunctions **119**
Ellipsis Omission or words easily understood **132**
Zeugma Sharing words, usually verbs, with conflicting nouns **134**
Syllepsis Sharing words that cause grammatical error **137**
Diazeugma One subject has many verbs **137**

DISRUPTION OF GRAMMAR
Hyperbaton Unusual word order **122**
Tmesis Splitting a word and often inserting an expletive **129**
Hendiadys Changing adjective and noun pair into two nouns **126**
Hypallage Placing an adjective with an inappropriate word **123**
Anthimeria Using one part of speech in place of another **127**
Anacoluthon Disrupting the flow of words and changing tack **123**

REPRESENTATION BY COMPARISON
Simile Explicit comparison of unrelated things **10**
Litotes Negative comparison of the opposite **73**
Metaphor Implied comparison by transference **26**

REPRESENTATION BY ASSOCIATION
Synecdoche Part for whole or whole for part **37**
Metonymy Thing represented by associated object or action **33**
Metalepsis Effect from a remote cause or tropes multiplied **52**
Merism Thing represented by listed parts or extremes **41**
Antonomasia Epithet used for name or name used for quality **45**
Epitheton Common attachment of an adjective to a name **47**

PERSONIFICATION
Personification Human qualities to non-living things **55**
Hypostatization Human qualities to abstractions **62**
Anthropomorphism Human qualities to creatures **60**
Zoomorphism Qualities of creatures to humans **60**

EXAGGERATION
Hyperbole Emphasis by exaggeration **48**
Synaesthesia Using one sense to experience another **53**
Catachresis Over-exaggerated or mixed metaphor **50**

UNDERSTATEMENT
Meiosis Understatement for emphasis **68**
Euphemism Making harsh words more palatable **69**
Dysphemism Using bad words either negatively or positively **71**
Litotes Understatement by negating the opposite **73**
Tapinosis Using understatement to belittle **72**

DOUBLE MEANING
Paradox An absurd idea makes sense **80**
Oxymoron Juxtaposition of contradictory ideas **81**
Paronomasia (Pun) Play on similar sounding words **88**
Antanaclasis Repeated use of homonyms **89**
Adianoeta Sentence with a subtle and opposite double meaning **89**

IRONIC OPPOSITION
Antiphrasis Ironic substitution of an opposite **87**
Antithesis Contrast of ideas in balanced phrases **85**

REPEATED SOUNDS
Consonance Repetition of consonant sounds **140**
Alliteration Rep. of cons. sounds at beginnings of words **141**
Paroemion Extreme alliteration **143**
Sibilance Repetition of sibilant sounds **143**
Assonance Repetition of vowel sounds **145**
Rhyme Similarity of emphasised vowel sounds **146**
Synathroesmus Repeated endings in a list of words **113**

DISCRETE SOUND
Dissonance A clash of sounds or rhythm **149**
Onomatopoeia Words imitate sounds of what they describe **150**

Works Quoted
alphabetically by author

Addison, Joseph; *The Campaign*
Alcott, Louisa May; *Little Women*
Aristophanes; *Frogs*
Austen, Jane; *Pride and Prejudice*
Browning, Elizabeth Barret; *Aurora Leigh*
Baudelaire, Charles; *Song of Autumn*
Blake, William; *The Marriage of Heaven and Hell; London,*
Brontë, Charlotte; *Jane Eyre*
Brontë, Emily; *Cold in th´ Earth; Fall Leaves Fall; Hope; Lines;
    Remembrance; Wuthering Heights*
Brown, George Douglas; *The House with the Green Shutters*
Browning, Robert; *Meeting at Night; Porphyria's Lover*
Buchan, John; *Prester John; The Thirty-Nine Steps; Witch Wood*
Burgess Gelett; *The Purple Cow*
Burns Robert *Address to the Deil; Jolly Beggars; To a Louse; No
    Churchman am I, Red Red Rose; Ronalds Of The
    Bennals; Scotch Drink; Tam O'Shanter*
Lord Byron, George Gordon; *Don Juan; She Walks in Beauty*
Carroll, Lewis; *Alice in Wonderland; Jabberwocky (Through the
    Looking Glass)*
Chesterton, G.K.; *Orthodoxy*
Coleridge, Samuel Taylor; *Constancy to an Ideal Object;
    Cristabel; Frost at Midnight; The Rime of the Ancient
    Mariner*
Doyle, Arthur Conan; *The Boscombe Valley Mystery; The Copper
    Beeches; The Engineer's Thumb; The Final Problem; The
    Five Orange Pips; The Hound of the Baskervilles; The
    Man with the Twisted Lip; The Noble Bachelor; A
    Scandal in Bohemia; The Sign of Four; The Speckled
    Band*
Congreve, William; *Amoret; Love for Love*
Conrad, Joseph; *Heart of Darkness; Lord Jim*
Crane, Stephen; *The Red Badge of Courage*

Dickens, Charles; *Bleak House; A Christmas Carol; David Copperfield; Great Expectations; Martin Chuzzlewit; Oliver Twist; The Pickwick Papers; A Tale of Two Cities*
Dickinson, Emily; *Almost!; The Bone that has no Marrow; "Hope" is the Thing with Feathers; The Soul selects her own Society; There's A Certain Slant Of Light; Under the Light, Yet Under,*
Donne, John: *Hymn to Christ*
Douglas Brown; *The House with the Green Shutters*
Dryden, John; *Absalom and Achitophel*
Eliot, George; *Adam Bede; Felix Holt; Middlemarch; The Mill on the Floss; Silas Marner*
Euripedes; *Medea*
Galt, John; *Ringan Gilhaizie*
Gilbert, W.S.; *The Nightmare*
Griffin, Bartholomew; *Fidessa, More Chaste Than Kinde*
Hardy, Thomas; *Tess of the d'Urbervilles*
Herrick, Robert; *To Dean Bourn*
Hogg, James; *The Brownie of Bodsbeck; Confessions of a Justified Sinner; The Three Perils of Man*
Hopkins, Gerard Manley; *Carrion Comfort; As Kingfishers Catch Fire*
James, Henry; *The Turn of the Screw*
Johnson, Samuel; *Rasselas; The Vanity of Human Wishes*
Joyce, James; *Dubliners; A Portrait of the Artist as a Young Man; Ulysses*
Keats, John; *To Autumn; To Hope; Ode on a Grecian Urn; Ode to a Nightingale;When I have Fears that I may Cease to Be*
Kingsley, Charles; *The Sands of Dee*
Kipling, Rudyard; *The Jungle Book*
Lawrence, D.H.; *Piano; Snake*
Lear, Edward; *The Owl and the Pussycat*
Lorca, Fredrico Garcia; *Cry from Rome; Moon and Panorama of the Insects*
Lovelace, Richard; *To Althea, from Prison*
Macpherson, James, *Ossain*
Marlowe, Christopher; *Doctor Faustus; The Jew of Malta*
Melville, Herman; *Bartleby, the Scrivener*
Milton, John; *Lycidas; Paradise Lost*

Mrs. Molesworth, Mary Louisa; *The Story of a Spring Morning*
Munro, Neil; *Para Handy; The Vital Spark*
O Henry; *Between Rounds; The Brief Debut of Tildy; ; Mammon and the Archer; The Romance of a Busy Broker; Sisters of the Golden Circle; The Skylight Room*
Orwell, George; *Animal Farm; Down and Out in Paris and London; Keep the Aspidistra Flying; Nineteen Eighty-Four; The Road to Wigan Pier*
Owen, Wilfrid; *Anthem for Doomed Youth; Dulce et Decorum Est; Strange Meeting*
Pepys, Samuel; *Diary*
Petronius; *Satyricon*
Poe, Edgar Allan; *Al-Aaraaf; Annabel Lee; Bells; Lenore; The Raven; Song; The Tell-Tale Heart*
Pope, Alexander; *Epistle to Dr. Arbuthnot; The Rape of the Lock*
Puttenham, George; *The Arte of English Poesie*
Rosenberg, Issac; *The Jew*
Rossetti, Christina; *A Birthday*
Runyon, Damon; *Barbecue; Big Shoulders; Broadway Incident; A Job for the Macarone; Johnny One-Eye; Leopard's Spots; A Light in France; Little Pinks; Maybe a Queen; The Melancholy Dane; Neat Strip; Old Em's Kentucky Home; A Piece of Pie; So You Wont Talk; Too Much Pep*
Schopenhauer, Arthur; *On the Suffering of the World*
Scott, Walter; *Heart of Midlothian; Ivanhoe; Marmion; Old Mortality*
Shakespeare, William; *Anthony and Cleopatra; As You Like It; Coriolanus; Cymbeline; Hamlet; Henry IV; Henry V; Henry VIII; Julius Caesar*; *King John*; *King Lear*; *Macbeth*; *Measure for Measure; The Merchant of Venice; A Midsummer Night's Dream; Othello; Richard II; Richard III; Romeo and Juliet; Sonnets 3;6;57;97;128; The Tempest; Troilus and Cressida; The Winter's Tale*
Shelley, Mary; *Frankenstein*
Shelley, Percy Bysshe; *Aziola; The Cloud; England in 1819; Euganean Hills; Hellas; Hymn to Intellectual Beauty; To Jane; To the Lord Chancellor; Love's Philosophy; The Mask of Anarchy; Prometheus Unbound; Rose Leaves; Stanzas Written in Dejection*

Smollett, Tobias; *The Expedition of Humphry Clinker*
Soutar, William; *The Guns*
Stein, Gertrude; *Susie Asado*
Stevenson, Robert Louis; *The Beach of Falesá; The Body-Snatcher; Catriona; The Ebb Tide; Kidnapped; Olalla; The Strange Case of Dr Jekyll and Mr Hyde; The Treasure of Franchard; The Wrecker*
Swift, Jonathan; *Gulliver's Travels; Tale of a Tub*
Tennyson, Alfred; *The Charge of the Light Brigade; Come Down, O Maid; The Eagle; The Lady of Shallot; Lancelot and Elaine; In Memoriam AHH; Morte D'Arthur; The Princess; Ulysses*
Twain, Mark; *Tom Sawyer*
Wells, H.G.; *The Time Machine*
Whitman, Walt; *Continuities; To a Locomotive in Winter; A Noiseless Patient Spider; Song of Myself*
Wilde, Oscar; *The Ballad of Reading Gaol; Lady Windermere's Fan; The Picture of Dorian Gray; Salome*
Woolf, Virginia; *Mrs Dalloway; To the Lighthouse; A Room of One's Own*
Wordsworth, William; *Daffodils; Tintern Abbey*
Yeats, William Butler; *Aedh Wishes for the Cloths of Heaven; Easter 1916; When You are Old*

General Quotes (not from specific works)
  Aeschines, Aeschylus, Dave Allen, Jane Austen, Muhammad Ali, Neil Armstrong, Francis Bacon, Cicero, Frederick Douglass, Henry Ford, Benjamin Franklin, Mahatma Gandhi, Alfred Hitchcock, Samuel Johnson, Immanuel Kant, Martin Luther King, J. F. Kennedy, Abraham Lincoln, Charles Rennie Mackintosh, Friedrich Nietzsche, Dorothy Parker, Punch, Paul Robeson, Boyle Roche, Eleanor Roosevelt, Jean Paul Sartre, George Bernard Shaw, Thucydides, Oscar Wilde, Thomas Wolfe

Index of Figures
(Main entries in capitals)

ADIANOETA 89
ALLITERATION 141
Anacoluthon 123, 134
ANADIPLOSIS 97
ANAPHORA 104
ANTANACLASIS 89
ANTHIMERIA 127
ANTHROPOMORPHISM 60
ANTIMETABOLE 102
ANTIPHRASIS 87
ANTITHESIS 85
ANTONOMASIA 45
Apostrophe 65, 134
ASSONANCE 145
ASYNDETON 119
BICOLON 114
CATACHRESIS 50
CHIASMUS 101
CONSONANCE 140
DIACOPE 94
DIAZEUGMA 137
DISSONANCE 149
DYSPHEMISM 71
ELLIPSIS 131–132
EPANALEPSIS 96
EPIPHORA 107
Epitheton 47
EPIZEUXIS 92
EUPHEMISM 69
HENDIADYS 126
HYPALLAGE 123
HYPERBATON 122
HYPERBOLE 48
HYPOSTATIZATION 62
HYPOTAXIS 121
Hypozeuxis 136
Hypozuegma 136

ISOCOLON   112
LITOTES   73
MEIOSIS   68
MERISM   41
MESODIPLOSIS   110
METALEPSIS   52
METAPHOR   26
METONYMY   33
Mezozuegma   136
ONOMATOPOEIA   150
OXYMORON   81
PARADOX   80
PARATAXIS   120
Paroemion   143
PARONOMASIA   88
PERSONIFICATION   55
POLYPTOTON   99, 128
POLYSYNDETON   117
Prozeugma   136
PUN   88
RHYME   146
SIBILANCE   143
SIMILE   10
SYLLEPSIS   131, 137
SYMPLOCE   108
SYNAESTHESIA   53
Synathroesmus   113
SYNECDOCHE   37
TAPINOSIS   72
TMESIS   129
TRICOLON   115
verbification   128
ZEUGMA   131, 134
ZOOMORPHISM   60